D1356755

# 100 years

## bob stoddard

# pepsi
## 100 years

GENERAL

PUBLISHING

GROUP

Los Angeles

Publisher: *W. Quay Hays*

Editorial Director: *Peter L. Hoffman*

Art Director: *Susan Anson*

Editor: *Amy Spitalnick*

Production Director: *Trudihope Schlomowitz*

Prepress Manager: *Bill Castillo*

Production Artist: *Gaston Moraga*

Production Assistants: *Tom Archibeque, David Chadderdon, Gus Dawson, Russel Lockwood, Regina Troyer*

Editorial Assistant: *Dana Stibor*

Copyeditors: *Steve Baeck, Mark Lamana, Dianne Woo*

Front Cover Concept: *Robert Avellan*

*For information:*
General Publishing Group, Inc.
2701 Ocean Park Boulevard, Suite 140
Santa Monica, CA  90405

Library of Congress Cataloging-in-Publication Data

Stoddard, Bob
    Pepsi  :  100 years / by Bob Stoddard.
        p.    cm.
    Includes index.
    ISBN 1-57544-026-1
    1. PepsiCo inc.        I. Title.
TP630.S76   1997
338.7′66362′0973—dc21

97-30663
CIP

Printed in the USA by RR Donnelley & Sons Company
10 9 8 7 6 5 4 3 2

GENERAL PUBLISHING GROUP
*Los Angeles*

# table of contents

# acknowledgments

The author wishes to thank the following individuals and organizations for their invaluable contributions to this book:

| | |
|---|---|
| Susan Stoddard | George Hunnicutt |
| John F. Minges | Walter Gross Jr. |
| Sarah Minges | Brantley Burnett |
| Hoyt Minges | Tom Burnett |
| Jerome Lapides | Stanley Goldberg |
| Kathy Hays | National Soft Drink Association |
| Sue Gustin | Stephanie Macceca |
| Jeff Powell | Library of Congress |
| John T. Minges | Virginia State Library |
| Ellen Zobrist | The Pepsi-Cola Company |
| Mark Zobrist | New Bern Public Library |
| Billy Pruden | Richard Gooding |
| George Bradham | Brad Richter |
| Walter Mack | Richard Dossin |
| Marie Hebbler | W.C. Jones |
| Bill Dimich | James Jessup Jr. |
| Maurice Irvin | Patty Chalovich |
| Dale Halton | Franklin Wright |

*This book is dedicated to the men and women of Pepsi-Cola*

*and the Pepsi family bottlers, who overcame many obstacles*

*in making Pepsi the success it is today.*

# introduction

## donald m. kendall

By the time Bob Stoddard handed me his manuscript, I'd already had a ringside seat in the Pepsi-Cola saga for 50 years.

I'd started with the company in 1947 selling syrup in New York. And I still spend most days joyfully laboring in the name of PepsiCo. So when it comes to Pepsi-Cola, I've heard all the stories, read all the history, and met all the people.

Or so I thought until I read Bob Stoddard's manuscript.

Bob has proved me wrong in the most delightful way. He has researched and written a truly insightful history, capable of enlightening even the most seasoned Pepsi-watcher. Ironically, his greatest triumph may be the remarkable color and detail with which he recounts the very early years—a period to which previous writers devoted scant attention.

By weaving together a rich array of facts and anecdotes, including some wonderful stories I'd never before heard, he has written a lively and engaging account of Pepsi's 100-year evolution.

The text reflects Bob's thousands of conversations with bottlers, industry executives, and others who have been witnesses to that evolution. Through them he has faithfully captured what has been a hallmark of Pepsi-Cola from the start: a will to win that has endured even in the bleakest times.

To this day, the Pepsi-Cola Company reflects to a remarkable degree the incredible passion of its founder, Caleb Bradham. As Bob vividly illustrates, Bradham was an entrepreneur in the most romantic sense: a man whose belief in his product was unshakable, and who relentlessly sought new and creative ways to sell it.

That belief made Caleb Bradham a marketing pioneer. He gladly gave away samples of his new drink—never doubting people would come back for more. And departing from the convention of the time, he used testimonials of real people in advertising—first his daughter Mary, then auto racer Barney Oldfield (possibly the first celebrity to endorse a product).

In fact, Bob Stoddard chronicles trailblazing throughout the history of Pepsi. Pepsi was, after all, the first company to use a musical "jingle" in advertising, the first to use animated characters in advertising, and the first to advertise its product from space.

Closest to my heart, though, is the historic effort that led up to Pepsi becoming the first western product produced in the Soviet Union. In describing that time, Bob conveys the unusual events that sometimes make or break big business deals.

Not every chapter in Pepsi's history ended in triumph, of course. The book captures in great detail the dramatic struggles of the early years that pushed Pepsi-Cola into bankruptcy more than once.

Somehow, though, Pepsi always came back. It never gave up. And in telling that story, Bob reveals both the heart and soul of successful enterprise. Perhaps most important, he illustrates the undeniable link between competition and greatness. In my opinion, without a great competitor over many years, Pepsi-Cola would be nowhere near the excellent company it is today. We owe a lot to "the other cola." And they owe a lot to us!

In fact, seldom are the benefits of competition clearer than in the soft drink industry. Competition has led to better products, better advertising, innovative packaging, and lower prices. In turn, that's led to higher soft drink consumption, higher sales, and higher profits. In other words, everybody wins.

I'm convinced free enterprise has been good for our country and for the world, too. Among the things I'm most proud of is the part Pepsi-Cola may have played in the downfall of Communism. I can't prove that Pepsi gave Eastern Bloc consumers their first taste of freedom, but I sure like to think so.

Over the years, hundreds of thousands of people have contributed to the success and greatness of Pepsi-Cola. I'm honored and pleased Bob Stoddard has chosen to tell their story.

*Former Chairman and*
*Chief Executive Officer*
*PepsiCo, Inc.*
*September 15, 1997*

9

# introduction

roger enrico

To me there's an intriguing irony about *Pepsi: 100 Years*. The book, of course, is a history, a retrospective, a look back—one that's both thorough and enlightening, even for a veteran of the business.

Yet, in a fundamental sense, it goes against the grain of Pepsi. You see, its colorful history notwithstanding, the Pepsi-Cola "family" is not naturally inclined to look back. We tend to focus on tomorrow rather than yesterday.

For better or for worse, we may be the least reflective organization on Earth.

We're 100 years old. Still, we do not have a museum. Our brand image evokes anything but "the good old days." Pepsi is almost synonymous with youth. And as a scrappy number two, we've always tried to keep things fresh and exciting and new.

It's not that we have anything against nostalgia. It's great—for other companies. But at Pepsi we don't think of our brand as any older than the day it was born.

Bob has traced a century of Pepsi-Cola's development in a way that entertains and educates. And I love a good history. But what struck me most about *Pepsi: 100 Years* maybe isn't surprising—that is, what it suggests about Pepsi's future.

You see, in delving into our past, Bob has done a remarkable job of bringing out the "personality" of the Pepsi-Cola family. He has brought to light the vital traits that propelled Pepsi through its first 100 years: the extraordinary optimism, ambition, resourcefulness, and perseverance.

These are the qualities that enabled Pepsi to withstand economic blows that would have destroyed many companies. They are the qualities that enabled Pepsi not just to survive, but to prosper against a much larger competitor.

As I see it, those enduring qualities that Bob Stoddard has highlighted are precisely what will enable us to flourish in the next century and well beyond.

In that respect, Bob's work is much more than a compelling history. It's a window into the future. By showing us the fundamental strengths of the Pepsi-Cola brand and the people who have dedicated themselves to building it, Bob has reinforced my own belief that the first 100 years of Pepsi-Cola are just the opening chapter of a long and very exciting story.

*Chairman and*
*Chief Executive Officer*
*PepsiCo, Inc.*
*October 9, 1997*

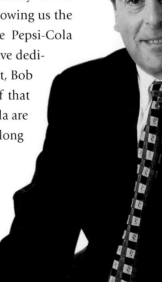

# exhilarating, invigorating, aids digestion

A devastating war far behind them and the seeds of technological marvels all around them, Americans in the Gay '90s ardently pursued their passions and ambitions. Their country, after all, had achieved wonders, linked by steel rails and girders and telephone wires to emerge by the dawn of the 20th century as the emerging industrial giant of the world. They had also outgrown a continent, amassing the overseas territories of Hawaii, American Samoa, Guam, Puerto Rico, and the Philippines. In the nation's physical and economic expansion, Americans saw the promise of boundless wealth and progress.

And, in the new-fashioned glow of electric light, optimism ran high. The industrial revolution had created thousands of jobs, and even economic panics—striking in 1873 and 1893—failed to deter a populace destined, so they believed, for prosperity. Businesses bounced back from the depressions left in the wake of the panics, and wages were on the rise. The rags-to-riches novels and serials of Horatio Alger Jr.—as well as such real-life stories as Andrew Carnegie starting out as a bobbin boy in a textile mill and ending up a steel magnate—spurred Americans, through hard work and (echoing one of Alger's titles) pluck, to try to join the 100 among them who, by 1889, were millionaires.

As Americans pursued their aspirations to wealth, so they did their vocation as consumers. From 1870 to 1900, while annual per capita income in the U.S. increased by more than 25 percent, the average workday decreased from 12 to 10 hours. With money in their pockets and time on their hands, and abetted by young, aggressive ad agencies, Americans were

*R.F. Butler in front of Bradham's Drug Store, where Pepsi-Cola was invented. Butler, known as Uncle Dick, took over operating the store when Bradham determined it was time to devote his efforts to making Pepsi-Cola a success.*

*Caleb Davis Bradham, inventor of Pepsi-Cola and founder of the Pepsi-Cola Company.*

*Right: Bradham in his North Carolina Naval Militia uniform.*

ready and willing buyers of novelties and embracers of trends.

A product for which numerous Americans at the turn of the century opened their hearts—and pocketbooks—falls into the general category of patent medicines. While technology was advancing on a number of fronts, medical treatment lagged far behind. Encouraged by advertisements offering elixirs for complaints as vague as fatigue and deadly as cancer, large numbers of the population put their hopes in—and money behind—these remedies, which were reassuringly reminiscent of popular folk cures. They offered an option, in any case, to the prospect of surgery, which at the time presented a high mortality rate.

Ingredients as exotic as ginseng and alarming as uranium were included in these tonics, sold by often-unscrupulous vendors, who disguised their potential dangers with benign product names like Capudine, Bilious Pills, and Mexican Sarsaparilla. A popular alternative to these potions was soda fountain drinks concocted by pharmacists. Soda water, long known for its digestive properties, was combined with a variety of ingredients including syrups to create drinks that were part refreshment, part tonic.

In many small towns of the late 1800s, the local pharmacist was the equivalent of a medical doctor, a university-trained physician being something of a rarity outside urban centers. It was thus left up to the town pharmacist to diagnose common ailments and even prescribe and dispense medications.

Moreover, the drugstore soda fountain was a place for

locals to gather at the end of the day and unwind with a drink that promised to refresh and revitalize. Of course, the revitalization in some of these drinks came from the addition of small amounts of cocaine, alcohol, and narcotics such as opium. One of the most popular soft drinks of the day, Coca-Cola, contained cocaine, at least until 1906—giving rise to the nickname dope, which was the term many people used when ordering the beverage.

Also during this time, claims pertaining to the health benefits of the coca leaf and kola nut circulated widely in various magazines and trade journals. Pharmacists were quick to pick up on the popularity of these ingredients and experiment with various concoctions of syrup. A few of these cola-type drinks became so popular they were patented and trademarked for mass distribution. Hence, the soft drink industry was born.

The Pepsi-Cola story itself begins with a drugstore in New Bern, North Carolina, and a pharmacist named Caleb Bradham. Bradham's aim was to create a fountain drink that was both delicious and healthful in aiding digestion and boosting energy. It would be free of the impurities found in many bottled health tonics, and it would contain none of the stronger narcotics often added to popular fountain drinks.

Years later, in an article printed in the Greensboro *Daily News* dated January 21, 1917, Bradham reflected on his motivation to invent Pepsi-Cola. A comment from his doctor about the harmful nature of many of the most popular fountain drinks of the day caused Bradham to muse, *Why can't I com-*

**Delicious Drinks.**

There's nothing better than our Soda Drinks—absolutely better. They are perfectly delicious. They are refreshing. They are real nourishment and in a form relished by everyone young and old.

BEAUX—the young lady would be impolite if she suggested that you come here, although she may prefer very much to come here with you for the Soda Drinks. Please her immensely by bringing her here. This is New Bern's Best Soda.

*Bradham's Prescription Pharmacy,*
Cola Headache Powders 10c.        NEW BERN, N. C.

*pound a drink that is good tasting, healthful, and refreshing?*

As did most pharmacies in 1896, Bradham's drugstore housed a soda fountain where the small-town clientele would meet to socialize. Bradham's establishment even featured a kind of primitive jukebox, which for a nickel would entertain the listener with the latest musical selections rendered by violin or piano or both. According to one patron, John Philip Sousa's legendary band hadn't anything on this device when it came down to a question of producing melody.

It was at such convivial gatherings that Bradham would offer his latest concoction. Over time, one of his recipes became known as Brad's Drink. A member of the press declared, "It has sparkle and just enough acidity to make it pleasant." Soon, its popularity would exceed the boundaries of New Bern.

*While Bradham regularly advertised the patent medicines available in his drugstore, he liked to promote his soda fountain as well.*

Bradham used his friends and neighbors as taste testers. Bradham is standing behind the bar, as he always did when mixing his special blends for the locals.

*Syrup bottles sat on the back bar where the fountain clerk could conveniently reach them to mix drinks.*

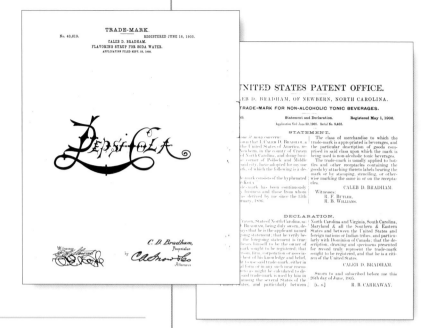

*Legend has it that the original Pepsi-Cola logo was drawn by Bradham's next-door neighbor. It was registered with the U.S. Patent Office in 1903, but there is no indication it was ever used.*

In the burgeoning soft drink industry, there was one giant and many small, under-financed competitors. The giant, Coca-Cola, got their start in 1886. By 1899, they were selling 280,000 gallons of syrup annually and spending $48,000 on advertising, marking their dominance in the fountain beverage business. Over the years, they became convinced they had exclusive right to the use of the word *cola* and were adamant that any other cola drink was nothing more than an imitation of Coca-Cola and were liable to be sued for trademark infringement.

Back in 1898, ready for the challenge and confident of success, Caleb Bradham prepared to join the ranks of the small, undercapitalized, overly enthusiastic competitors of Coca-Cola. That year, Bradham began to market Brad's Drink, renamed Pepsi-Cola, to other drugstores.

Although no existing accounts verify the origin of the name, it is generally believed that Pepsi was derived from pepsin, an enzyme that aids digestion—not because Pepsi-Cola contained pepsin, but because it was believed that the beverage likewise aided the digestive process. Contrary to the implications of the word *cola*, the original formulation of Pepsi-Cola did not contain the kola nut, only a refreshing cola taste, which many believed revitalized them when tired.

The cellar of Bradham's drugstore served as the original site of Pepsi-Cola syrup manufacture. Electing to start his new business on a small, manageable scale, Bradham based his operation on familiar territory. Ingredients were hauled downstairs to cramped quarters where they were mixed together and then cooked in a large kettle. The syrup was subsequently poured into one-gallon jugs and five-gallon kegs to be shipped to customers.

By 1902, the demand from surrounding drugstores increased so dramatically it dawned on Bradham that Pepsi-Cola was something special. On December 24, 1902, he filed incorporation papers with the state of North Carolina; in these, he indicated his plans for corporate branches in Virginia, Maryland, Pennsylvania, and New York. Also stated was the corporate objective: to manufacture and sell a soda fountain syrup known as Pepsi-Cola, and to manufacture and deal in soda fountain drinks and specialties.

At this point, Bradham believed the Pepsi-Cola Company would service only the soda fountain trade. Bradham named himself president, with 98 shares of the new company's stock. Friends R.F. Butler and B.G. Credle had one share each. The total value of the shares at this time was $10,000, and the incorporation papers limited stock value to $100,000. This relatively low dollar amount for corporation assets suggests that Bradham's goals at the time were comparatively modest, focusing strictly on the fountain trade. He was yet to consider selling a bottled, carbonated soft drink.

Nevertheless, with the increasing popularity of Pepsi-Cola, Bradham grew concerned with guarding his formula. On September 23, 1902, he applied to the U.S. Patent Office for a trademark that would protect the Pepsi-Cola name and formula. On the application, Bradham stated that the Pepsi-Cola name had been in continuous use since August 1, 1901. In fact, a company in New Jersey already owned a similar trademark. The name Pep-Kola had been registered by A.W. Stewart and Co. on June 23, 1896, and was subsequently sold to the Alphasol Company. As a result, Bradham's initial trademark application for Pepsi-Cola was rejected.

To remedy this problem, Bradham purchased the Pep-Kola trademark from the Alphasol Company for $100. Pepsi-Cola then legally became the trademark descendant of Pep-Kola. This would later cause a good deal of confusion in determining the actual starting date of Pepsi-Cola. Each incarnation of the company used a different date to mark the beginning of Pepsi-Cola. Indeed, not until the 1940s would 1898 be established as the year Pepsi-Cola actually began.

While waiting for approval from the U.S. Patent Office of his Pepsi-Cola trademark, Bradham decided to also register the trademark with the state of North Carolina. In his application to the state, Bradham claimed the Pepsi-Cola trademark had been in use since August 28, 1898, which is traditionally held to be the date Pepsi-Cola was launched. The U.S. Patent Office finally granted Pepsi-Cola its first trademark in 1903, but for inexplicable reasons this trademark was never used. A modified version of the first trademark was approved on August 7, 1906.

*The Pepsi-Cola logo registered in 1906 has been used ever since in numerous versions.*

*From 1902, the earliest known Pepsi-Cola advertisement.*

**PEPSI-COLA**

HEALTHFUL AND INVIGORATING.

Cures Nervousness, Relieves Exhaustion, Promotes Digestion.

**5c.**

AT SODA FOUNTAINS.

AT ALL SODA FOUNTAINS.

Delicious, Healthful, Refreshing and Invigorating. The most Cooling and Satisfying.

**5c.**

*Right: The Pepsi-Cola script logo was first used February 25, 1903, in the* Weekly Journal, *New Bern's local newspaper.*

*Pepsi-Cola syrup was originally sold in gallon jugs.*

Pepsi-Cola's earliest advertising was by word of mouth. Visitors to New Bern would return home raving about this wonderful new drink called Pepsi-Cola. The first newspaper advertisements appeared in 1902 in the *New Bern Weekly Journal*. Although Pepsi-Cola was never intended to be a patent medicine, these first ads point to the medicinal benefits of the drink. Under captions reading THE PEPSIN DRINK, they maintain that Pepsi-Cola "aids digestion, cures headaches, and dispels that tired feeling."

Throughout those early years, Pepsi presented itself as a product offering good-tasting refreshment that also provided health benefits. As one description of Pepsi-Cola trumpeted, the ingredients are those that stimulate digestion, relieve the tired nerves, and in fact is the most unique, refreshing bouquet that ever delighted the palate. Notably, these earliest advertisements displayed the Pepsi-Cola name in standard block print, the famous stylized Pepsi-Cola script not being featured until February 1903.

With sales of Pepsi-Cola increasing—from sales of 2,000 gallons of syrup in 1902 to 8,000 gallons a year later, Bradham could no longer manufacture enough Pepsi-Cola syrup from his drugstore basement to meet the demand. To solve this admittedly

welcome dilemma, Bradham purchased the Bishop factory, which would become the first home office of the Pepsi-Cola Company.

At this time, Pepsi-Cola was sold by the glass at soda fountains primarily in North Carolina. And, since the early days of soft drinks being sold at soda fountains, the established price was five cents for a six-ounce glass. While occasionally, a competitor would undercut this price or economic conditions would force the price up temporarily, eventually the price would return to the nickel consumers had come to expect.

Soft drinks in bottles were comparatively rare in the late 1800s due to the cost and limited availability of handblown glass. Bottles were still made by hand, and the closure system consisting of a stopper held in place by a piece of wire was less than efficient. The seal was often far from complete, releasing the carbonation.

Fortunately for Bradham and Pepsi-Cola, the soft drink industry was on the verge of revolutionary changes. In the early 1900s, equipment was developed that would automate the manufacture of glass bottles. Almost simultaneously, William Painter had perfected a new closure system that not only was easy to use but also offered a perfect seal just about every time. The key to Painter's system was that manufactured bottles were nearly always

consistent in size and shape, enabling the caps to fit tightly. This new closure, eventually referred to as the pop bottle cap, could even be imprinted to identify the product inside.

Bradham, visionary that he was, sensed that bottles could advance the soft drink trade by attracting customers in areas without soda fountains. The rural consumer offered a large, untapped, and far-flung market for Pepsi-Cola that could only be reached by offering the beverage in bottles. To take advantage of what he believed consumers would soon demand, Bradham offered bottled Pepsi-Cola in New Bern. A bottling line was added in the new plant being built for syrup manufacture.

Bottling soft drinks at this stage was more an art than a science. The product just might explode during the capping process, thanks to inconsistencies in the glass bottles and the differing carbonation levels. Workers on the bottling line were therefore outfitted with protective equipment, primitive though it was by today's safety standards.

Bradham's Pepsi-Cola bottling plant was clearly blazing a trail in the soft drink trade. Many existing bottling operations were merely one-man operations. Bradham, however, was using the latest equipment to produce Pepsi-Cola in assembly-line fashion.

The conversion of the Bishop factory to the Pepsi-Cola plant began in September 1904. On April 5, 1905, the new home office was open to the public for inspection, with each guest receiving a sample bottle. Bradham believed that plant tours assured the public of Pepsi-Cola's quality, and built goodwill in the community.

Convinced that bottles would play a significant role in Pepsi-Cola's future, Bradham ordered half a million be delivered by the time the new plant opened. Meanwhile, besides changing how Pepsi-Cola could be purchased, bottling would alter the nature of the Pepsi-Cola Company. In addition to selling Pepsi to the fountain trade, Bradham would also need to develop a network of Pepsi-Cola bottlers to bottle and promote the product.

At the time, independent soft drink bottlers were many, and most bottled soft drinks were locally derived and distributed, becoming popular regionally. To be successful, Bradham would need to persuade these local, independent bottlers to concentrate their efforts on Pepsi-Cola. Otherwise, Pepsi-Cola's expansion would remain limited.

*An early syrup dispenser*

*design. An ounce of*

*syrup and five ounces of*

*carbonated water made*

*a glass of Pepsi-Cola.*

Bayard Wootten 1908

Bradham was taking a big risk here. Still in its infancy, soft drink bottling had not yet proved its worth. The industry leader, Coca-Cola, not considering bottling to be important, had given the rights to bottle their product to a couple of entrepreneurs from Tennessee.

But Bradham's gamble paid off. By 1907, Pepsi-Cola syrup sales had increased from almost 20,000 gallons in 1904 to over 100,000 gallons. Ever the visionary, Bradham began to think beyond North Carolina to the possibility of selling Pepsi-Cola worldwide. He promptly registered the Pepsi-Cola trademark in Canada and in Mexico.

*Above: The Pepsi-Cola logo, 1907.*

*Far left: The first Pepsi-Cola bottle design.*

*The home office and bottling plant of Pepsi-Cola was three stories high. Visible throughout New Bern, it soon became a local landmark.*

Bradham's ambitions faced the formidable challenge of running a large business from a small town. Because access to capital is vital to the growth of a business, especially when cash flow is limited, the lack of financial institutions in New Bern made expansion difficult. Bradham was often forced to go outside New Bern for loans and financial assistance. Moreover, the railroads in and out of New Bern had limited schedules, thus hampering timely deliveries, and the roads were not amenable to trucks carrying heavy loads.

What Bradham did to push past such limitations included hiring a crack sales team and setting up an effective bottler network. Judging that securing bottlers was vital to Pepsi's development, by late 1905, Bradham started licensing bottlers in North Carolina.

One of the first cities to receive a Pepsi-Cola franchise was Charlotte. The Charlotte Pepsi-Cola Bottling Company was incorporated in North Carolina on November 16, 1905. Of the company's initial officers J.J. Adams, Geo. H. Brockenbrough, H.B. Fowler, and C.C. Kennedy, only H.B. Fowler's family still operates the Charlotte Pepsi-Cola Bottling Company.

The early bottler faced many obstacles in building up his Pepsi-Cola franchise, chief among them transportation. Pepsi-Cola bottlers relied primarily on trains for shipping their product to outlying communities, while horse-drawn wagons delivered to local customers. At the time, only a few gas-powered delivery trucks were found in the Carolinas. Charlotte became not only one of the first cities to bottle Pepsi but also one of the first to use a motor-driven delivery vehicle.

By the end of 1906, the Pepsi-Cola Company had franchised 15 bottling plants. The fountain side of the business was also expanding, due in part to Pepsi's reputation for being a pure product. Many soft drinks of the day contained harmful substances such as arsenic, barium, lead, cadmium, and uranium. In 1905, the state of North Carolina passed a law banning these harmful materials from food and beverages. The federal government followed suit in 1906 with the Pure Food and Drug Act, forcing many soft drink manufacturers to remove narcotics and other harmful ingredients from their products. While Coca-Cola was forced to change their formula to be in compliance with the law, Pepsi-Cola, being free of any such impurities, was able to claim they already met federal requirements.

Indeed, because of their product's absolute purity, Pepsi adopted the slogan PURE FOOD DRINK in 1907. Bradham believed so completely in Pepsi-Cola's purity that he advertised it as safe even for children—something not many of his competitors could honestly claim.

"OUR PLANT"

PEPSI-COLA

Charlotte Pepsi-Cola Co.

From 1906 to 1907, the Pepsi-Cola Company principally advertised in newspapers and on walls. Painting crews would travel throughout a state, emblazoning Pepsi-Cola on any wall where they'd received permission to do so. Pepsi-Cola also gave away an assortment of promotional novelties, including serving trays, straw holders, and tip trays that today are worth thousands of dollars.

The following year, Pepsi-Cola obtained their first celebrity endorsement. Famed race car driver Barney Oldfield appeared in a Pepsi-Cola newspaper ad in 1908, declaring, "I enjoy Pepsi-Cola first rate. It's a bully drink—refreshing, invigorating, a fine bracer before a race, and a splendid restorer afterwards."

*Charlotte, North Carolina, was home to the first Pepsi-Cola bottler licensed by Bradham.*

*Workers bottling Pepsi-Cola at the Memphis, Tennessee, plant in 1908. The equipment was considered state of the art, even though only about 60 cases could be produced in an hour. Today, most bottling equipment can easily produce that amount in a minute.*

*One of the early motor-driven vehicles used to deliver Pepsi-Cola was owned by Charlotte Pepsi-Cola.*

*Every bottle of Pepsi-Cola was supposed*

*to have a label affixed to it, but was*

*often left off for speed and convenience.*

*Bradham believed so*

*completely in the health*

*benefits and purity*

*of Pepsi-Cola that,*

*in advertisements,*

*children were seen*

*drinking it. Of course,*

*Pepsi-Cola did not*

*contain caffeine*

*at the time.*

C.D.BRADHAM, President.    J.D.FARRIOR, Vice President.    R.F.BUTLER, Secretary.

THE PEPSI-COLA-CO.

MANUFACTURERS OF

DRINK Pepsi-Cola 5¢

DELICIOUS-HEALTHFUL

TRADE MARK REGISTERED

Refreshing, Invigorating. A Concentrated Syrup for Fountains & Bottler's use.

HOME OFFICE NEW BERN, N.C.

Dear Madam:

 Allow us to introduce to you little Miss Emma Hazeltine Woodley, the charming eight-months-old daughter of Mr. and Mrs. M. M. Woodley of Lancaster, S. C.  Early in life, several months ago we should say, this little lady learned that there is no drink like Pepsi-Cola and she has been drinking it daily since that time.

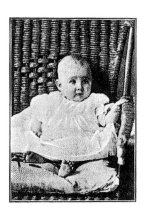

 That it agrees with her is evidenced by the accompanying picture. She is as fat as a butterball, has a disposition as sunny as the clime of Italy and is growing stronger and prettier as the days go by.

 Mr. and Mrs. Woodley say that Pepsi-Cola did it.  Little Miss Emma can't talk yet but when she grows old enough, she will daily give praise to this delicious beverage.

 The above is said seriously and by request of Mr. and Mrs. Woodley who realize fully their moral responsibility in declaring Pepsi-Cola an absolutely harmless, wholesome beverage, delightful, refreshing, nourishing and beneficial to young and old.

 Ask your doctor.  He knows.

 Give the children all they can hold.  Pepsi-Cola is downright good for their health.  Order it by the case; it is an economical custom now well established in the best of homes--twenty-four bottles cost only ninety cents.

   Yours truly,

    THE PEPSI-COLA BOTTLING WORKS.

*Above: An early example of advertising by local bottlers, from Charlotte, North Carolina.*

*Race car driver Barney Oldfield was Pepsi-Cola's first celebrity endorser.*

*Sides of buildings were a popular place to display advertising messages in the early*

*1900s. The owner usually charged a fee based on how good the location was.*

With growth and expansion came the need for more capital. In order to amass the necessary funds without incurring debt, Bradham brought in an investor, a J.D. Farrior. Receiving half of the issued shares of Pepsi-Cola stock, Farrior became the company's first vice president. It was also reported in the *Southern Carbonator and Bottler* that Farrior obtained a half-interest in the Pepsi-Cola formula.

By 1907, annual Pepsi-Cola syrup sales had surpassed the 100,000-gallon mark, amounting to more than a 10-fold increase in just four years, with at least 40 percent of the increase resulting from the growth of the bottling side of the business. Pepsi-Cola was quickly outgrowing the Bishop factory, where it had moved just two years earlier. Bradham purchased the adjacent land and began construction on a three-story edifice that would eventually connect to the old building. Pepsi-Cola's new facility became such a noted landmark in New Bern that a postcard was issued to commemorate the town's distinction as home to Pepsi-Cola.

With sales increasing outside the Carolinas, Bradham determined that to facilitate growth, Pepsi needed regional representation. In 1908, the Pepsi-Cola Company of Memphis, Tennessee, opened as a branch office of the parent company. Its purpose was to distribute Pepsi-Cola syrup to plants in the surrounding area and to solicit new bottlers while promoting Pepsi-Cola throughout the region. It also bottled Pepsi-Cola for the Memphis area.

By the end of 1908, with more than 250 bottlers in 24 states licensed to bottle Pepsi-Cola, Bradham's dream of people imbibing his product from coast to coast was beginning to materialize.

# caleb davis bradham

Caleb Davis Bradham was born May 27, 1867, in Chinquapin, North Carolina, the son of George Washington and Julia McCann Bradham. Upon graduating the University of North Carolina, the compassionate young man determined to study medicine at the University of Maryland in hopes of becoming a doctor and alleviating people's suffering. As a medical student he worked part time apprenticing for a pharmacist at a local drugstore. This piqued his interest in tinkering with chemistry toward the goal of treating medical ailments.

A family financial crisis forced the ever-conscientious Bradham to abandon his medical training. Relocating to New Bern, North Carolina, he took a job teaching high school. A year later, Bradham redirected his energies to commerce and, eventually, hearing news that a local drugstore owner had died, Bradham entered into a business partnership to take over the concern. He was on the verge of fulfilling his ambition to promote people's well-being—this time as a pharmacist, concocting and dispensing healthful potions. In July 1895, Bradham passed the Board of Pharmacy exam, earning the second-highest grade of all the applicants that year.

Bradham was soon the sole owner of the drugstore. Here, Bradham created the numerous medicines he sold to local patrons in bottles proudly imprinted with "Bradham Drug Co." A special feature of his prescription department was a case ominously marked with a skull and crossbones, which, when opened by an unauthorized individual, sounded an alarm.

Bradham's drugstore was also where he

Bradham after his retirement, just a few years before he died.

created the product he would become most noted for—Pepsi-Cola. Pepsi-Cola became an overnight sensation. Within 10 years, Bradham's product was available in 24 states.

On January 1, 1901, Bradham married Charity Credle of New Bern. The daughter of B.G. Credle of New Bern, the bride had been working as a nurse in Philadelphia. Mr. Credle not only gained a son-in-law, but also received a share in the Pepsi-Cola Company. Soon after their marriage, the Bradhams started a family, their first child, Mary, being born in 1903, followed by Caleb Jr. in 1905 and George in 1907.

Bradham, meanwhile, demonstrated his deep sense of community responsibility by devoting his time to numerous civic groups and organizations, including the Masons and the Elks. He served as vice president of the People's Bank of New Bern, president of the state-owned railroad, and rear admiral of the North Carolina Naval Militia, which he helped found. At one point, he was even touted as a candidate for governor of North Carolina.

Due to a series of financial miscalculations, Bradham and the Pepsi-Cola Company were forced into bankruptcy by 1923. After the bankruptcy, Bradham, undaunted, returned to operating his drugstore and busily serving the community of New Bern. While the Pepsi-Cola enterprise had slipped from his grasp, his idealism and social conscience remained with him his whole life.

On February 19, 1934, Caleb Davis Bradham died after a long illness, never, sadly, to know the phenomenal success his beloved Pepsi-Cola would achieve.

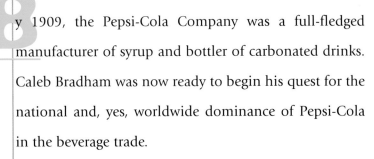

# delicious,
# and healthful

By 1909, the Pepsi-Cola Company was a full-fledged manufacturer of syrup and bottler of carbonated drinks. Caleb Bradham was now ready to begin his quest for the national and, yes, worldwide dominance of Pepsi-Cola in the beverage trade.

Consequently, Pepsi's advertising budget jumped from a little over $1,800 in 1903 to almost $66,000 by 1909. The advertising firm of Biggs, Young, Shone, and Co. of New York City was engaged to distinguish the soft drink from that of its less scrupulous competitors. A great deal of money subsequently funded high-quality advertising of Pepsi-Cola at fountains—the thousands of trays Pepsi gave away to soda fountain operators during this period have become some of the most cherished Pepsi collectibles.

To promote the sale of bottled Pepsi-Cola, several schemes were carried out, including a bottle cap redemption program. Dubbed Save the Caps, this was among Pepsi-Cola's first large-scale promotions. Catalogs were issued containing everything from pocket-knives to pianos, adding to consumers'

incentive to choose Pepsi and choose it often. The caps, when collected in sufficient amounts, could be redeemed from Pepsi-Cola for desired items.

Individual bottlers also devised their own promotions. One such promotion was linked with a local beauty pageant. Consumers could vote for their favorite contestant by dropping their collected bottle caps in a bucket placed under her likeness.

Early bottling territories were relatively small at the time, based as they were on the bottler's ability to service an area. The horse-drawn wagon being the primary delivery vehicle, the range of delivery was limited to how far a wagon loaded with bottles could travel to and from the plant in a single day.

By 1910, Pepsi-Cola had expanded

*Above: Before the advent of air conditioners, handheld fans were popular advertising items.*

*Opposite: Higher-quality advertising signs became commonplace with Pepsi's increasing popularity. Somewhat presumptuously, this sign calls Pepsi-Cola THE AMERICAN BEVERAGE.*

their bottling network to include 250 bottlers. Although this number may seem large, in reality it wasn't. Many, rather than serving exclusively as Pepsi bottlers, were instead wholesale grocers who became affiliated with Pepsi as a way to expand their grocery business. Others bottled Pepsi-Cola as simply one of many flavored drinks they produced. Still others were merely distributing to an area they had subfranchised from a nearby Pepsi-Cola bottler. In some cases, these distributors were so successful they would eventually open their own bottling plant. Fortunately, because enough bottlers made Pepsi the focus of their business and actively promoted the product, the Pepsi-Cola Company enjoyed significant growth.

To meet the needs of his growing enterprise, Bradham looked beyond the the local labor force to employ people who had experience operating a large business—people such as Edgar Gaines, who through his association with Charlotte Pepsi bottler H.B. Fowler became a Pepsi bottler in Gaffney, South Carolina. When Bradham learned that Gaines had been a regional manager with R.J. Reynolds Tobacco Co., he offered him a position as sales manager for the Pepsi-Cola Company.

Gaines' job was to increase fountain business and oversee development of the bottling business, everything from adding new bottlers to helping existing bottlers expand. Gaines hired regional representatives who could assist local bottlers in ensuring that Pepsi-Cola was bottled so that the flavor would match Bradham's intention, as well as checking that the plants were clean and sanitary.

*Straw holders, one of many promotional items used to entice soda fountain operators to sell Pepsi-Cola, were given away in 1909. Today, each is valued at more than $7,000.*

The cleanliness of bottling plants was a major concern in the early 1900s. Many people avoided buying soft drinks in bottles because of suspicions regarding sanitary conditions in some plants. Improperly

cleaned bottles, it was feared, could end up on store shelves. Indeed, newspapers published reports of consumers falling ill from dirty bottles traced to plants with lax sanitation standards. Reputations further suffered from the competition between fountain operators and bottlers. Soda fountain operators, alarmed at the damage to their business from bottled soft drink sales, readily exploited exposés appearing in the press.

*At a gathering of Pepsi-Cola salesmen, there are enough bottles of Pepsi-Cola on the table to satisfy everyone's thirst.*

*Many Pepsi-Cola bottlers took advantage of local parades to advertise Pepsi-Cola. This practice is still alive and well among some bottlers.*

*With the expansion of the Pepsi-Cola bottlers' business, more advertising material featured the Pepsi bottle.*

*During the early 1900s, communication between the parent Pepsi-Cola Company and their bottlers was highly inefficient, making a 1910 bottlers convention a necessity. Ideas and information were shared, and unity and amity fostered.*

Like bottles, improperly washed fountain glasses were also vehicles for spreading germs. Occasionally, local authorities would be forced to cite a soda fountain for not sanitizing glasses properly. In one case, the fine was as high as $2, the equivalent of a $30 to $40 fine today.

To counteract the public's suspicions, Pepsi held their bottlers to the strictest sanitation procedures of the time. They went so far as to urge bottlers to allow the public to tour plants to see firsthand that Pepsi was bottled under clean and sanitary conditions. Some bottlers were so wary of their image, they embossed the word *sanitary* on their bottles.

Also embossed on some bottles were the names of cities hosting bottling plants. In the early days of the soft drink industry, unscrupulous individuals went from town to town stealing bottles and selling them in a neighboring county or state. An honor system was in operation whereby route sales-

men would deliver a shipment of Pepsi-Cola and at the same time pick up the empties and return them to the plant to be cleaned and refilled. As bottles represented a significant outlay of cash for the bottler, in order to get a proper return on his investment, the bottler had to figure on using them hundreds of times. Bottlers who were vandalized were forced to lessen their inventory until they could afford to buy more bottles. Branding their bottles with the cities where their plants were located assured bottlers of laying claim to their property.

Although some states passed tough laws against bottle theft, such regulations had little effect without a federal ordinance prohibiting the stolen bottles from crossing state lines. Thus began the practice of charging deposits on bottles. This solution had the added benefit of providing consumers an opportunity to earn spending money by collecting bottles and turning them in for the deposit.

An excursion aboard the Elfrida was a pleasant getaway from the many serious issues discussed at the 1910 Pepsi-Cola Bottlers Convention.

Far left: Bradham believed that licensing bottlers was the key to making Pepsi-Cola America's choice from coast to coast.

### LICENSE TO BOTTLE PEPSI-COLA.

Left: The very first financial agreements granting permission to bottle Pepsi-Cola were nothing more than pieces of paper. Shortly thereafter, a formal license agreement was instituted.

Facing an assortment of issues in an industry still in its infancy, bottlers needed a way to share information and in some cases use their collective strength to solve problems. Simultaneously, Bradham sensed the benefit of forging far-flung, independent Pepsi-Cola bottlers into a unity, like a family. Pepsi-Cola thus planned its first bottlers convention. The event was held June 20–22, 1910, in Pepsi's hometown of New Bern, North Carolina.

This first convention was a splendid occasion, symbolizing as it did the hopes and dreams of Caleb Bradham himself that through the licensing of bottlers, Pepsi would become a national beverage. These bottlers, like missionaries, would carry the Pepsi-Cola message to a thirsty public. Pepsi bottlers from 24 different states were present, as well as representatives from various suppliers and the entire management of the Pepsi-Cola Company.

The bottlers were greeted by Bradham at the opening session. In addition, A.D. Ward, general legal counsel to the Pepsi-Cola Company, promised he would represent bottlers in any litigation involving Pepsi-Cola. A number of suppliers addressed the proper use of equipment and recent innovations. Most significant were the business and promotional tips from the bottlers themselves. Some speakers described how to improve the bottling process, while others told of how various contests and promotions had boosted sales. Many touted the benefits of advertising in local newspapers.

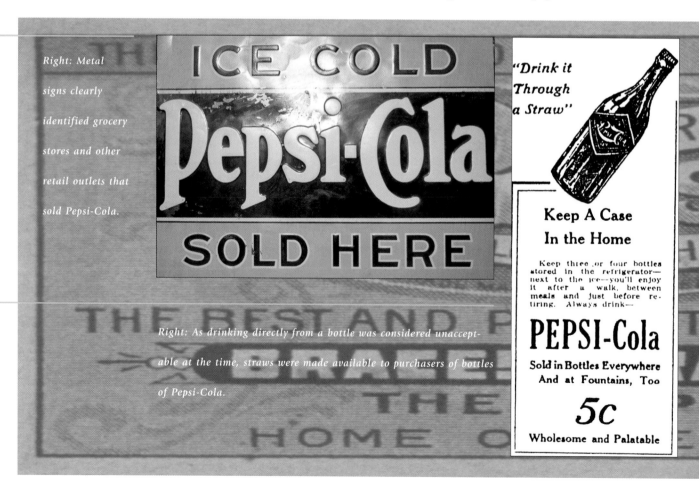

*Right: Metal signs clearly identified grocery stores and other retail outlets that sold Pepsi-Cola.*

ICE COLD
Pepsi-Cola
SOLD HERE

*Right: As drinking directly from a bottle was considered unacceptable at the time, straws were made available to purchasers of bottles of Pepsi-Cola.*

"Drink it Through a Straw"

Keep A Case In the Home

Keep three or four bottles stored in the refrigerator—next to the ice—you'll enjoy it after a walk, between meals and just before retiring. Always drink—

PEPSI-Cola

Sold in Bottles Everywhere And at Fountains, Too

5c

Wholesome and Palatable

Other activities at the convention included a tour of the Pepsi plant, pointing out the sanitary conditions required for properly producing the syrup. Bottlers were also treated to a cruise aboard the *Elfrida*, a ship owned by the North Carolina Naval Militia. (The ship was commanded by a member of the militia who also happened to be president of the Pepsi-Cola Company: Caleb Bradham.) Following the cruise, everyone was invited to an oyster roast hosted by the Crown, Cork, and Seal Co., suppliers of Pepsi-Cola bottle caps. Bottlers left the convention highly motivated and confident in their ability to promote Pepsi-Cola.

At the Second Annual Pepsi-Cola Bottlers Convention, held January 19–21, 1911, Bradham stressed the family concept of the company. He emphasized the benefits of the bottlers and the parent company working together as a cohesive unit.

The third annual convention, scheduled for January 1912, produced a formal association, the National Association of Pepsi-Cola Bottlers. Its purpose was to provide promotional assistance, encouragement, and ideas for advancing the bottling trade. J. Zeb Waller of Burlington, North Carolina, was elected its first president.

According to reports by the bottlers, the following year, 1913, was a highly successful one. In business just over two years, the Lancaster, South Carolina, plant showed a whopping 628 percent increase in sales. Other plants were showing gains of over 200 percent. Based on these sales figures, Pepsi-Cola's future looked promising indeed.

It's a magic charm—that name! Just try it at any fount — say PEPSI-Cola and watch the Cousin of the North Pole come in a long, thin dewy, "ice-bergy" glass. Go say "PEPSI-Cola" and treat yourself to the finest drink ever. And then 'phone your grocer for a case of PEPSI-Cola to be left *home*.

*Left: From 1910 to 1915, Pepsi-Cola advertising appeared regularly in newspapers wherever the soft drink was sold. One series of ads appealed to the season.*

*Left: The Gibson-style girl was one of the most popular images used in Pepsi-Cola advertising, gracing cardboard signs, serving trays, and straw holders.*

Attendees of the
Sixth Annual Bottlers
Convention cluster around
a Pepsi-Cola delivery
truck with Bradham
behind the wheel.

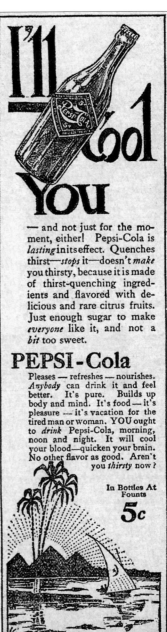

**I'll Cool You**

— and not just for the moment, either! Pepsi-Cola is *lasting* in its effect. Quenches thirst—*stops* it—doesn't *make* you thirsty, because it is made of thirst-quenching ingredients and flavored with delicious and rare citrus fruits. Just enough sugar to make *everyone* like it, and not a *bit* too sweet.

**PEPSI-Cola**

Pleases — refreshes — nourishes. *Anybody* can drink it and feel better. It's pure. Builds up body and mind. It's food — it's pleasure — it's vacation for the tired man or woman. YOU ought to *drink* Pepsi-Cola, morning, noon and night. It will cool your blood—quicken your brain. No other flavor as good. Aren't you *thirsty* now?

In Bottles At Founts

**5c**

Thematic advertising, including

a series utilizing the slogan

I'LL COOL YOU, helped Pepsi-Cola

develop a consistent image

and message.

*Gradually, trucks replaced the horse-drawn wagons that delivered Pepsi-Cola and became a central part of the company's bottling business.*

Curiously, Coca-Cola never challenged Pepsi-Cola's use of their trademark. It certainly wasn't because Coca-Cola was shy about accusing soft drink companies that used the word *cola* of violating Coke's trademark. In fact, many cola companies without the financial resources to defend themselves against this charge either sold out or closed up. It remains a mystery why Coca-Cola never contended Bradham's use of the Pepsi-Cola name.

One explanation lies in Bradham's association with Senator F.M. Simmons. Simmons, elected to the U.S. Senate in 1900, was from New Bern. A close personal friend of Bradham's, he had partnered the founder of Pepsi in a number of farming ventures. Any legal attacks on Bradham's drink, the theory goes, would launch a federal investigation into Coca-Cola's business practices, spearheaded by none other than Senator Simmons.

Coca-Cola had reason to fear such scrutiny. The year was 1911, the place, Chattanooga, Tennessee, the trial, *The United States* v. *Forty Barrels and Twenty Kegs of Coca-Cola.* The government charged Coca-Cola with violation of the pure food law, specifically, incorrect labeling of ingredients. The trial dragged on until 1917, when Coca-Cola pleaded no contest in order to settle the case. In 1916, meanwhile, the Federal Trade Commission had targeted Coca-Cola's trade practices for investigation. At issue was the company's refusal to sell Coca-Cola to dealers who handled competing brands and threats of lawsuits against competitors.

On June 28, 1914, Archduke Francis Ferdinand was assassinated in the city of Sarajevo, Bosnia, triggering World War I. A continent away in the small town of New Bern, North Carolina, people worried how their lives would be affected. In fact, unforeseen at the time, the war would cause sugar shortages and the implementation of a government policy

**UNCLE SAM**

And the People of The United States

Are Standing Together in Their Declaration
That *Pepsi-Cola* is the National Beverage

Buy It
By the
Crate

**The People Have Declared War**

On all substitutes---demanding the genuine
product---that good old *Pepsi-Cola* which
bubbles over with deliciousness as each
crown is taken off.

Ask your dealer to avail himself of our efficient truck delivery service which supplies not
only Winston-Salem, but nearby towns and adjacent territory, for everybody wants delicious
and healthful *Pepsi-Cola*---Every bottle thoroughly sterilized.

**Pepsi-Cola Bottling Co.**

West Third Street          Phone 626          Van B. Melchor, Mgr.

*Far left: Patriotic advertising by businesses in times of national crisis is an American tradition, honored by Pepsi-Cola during World War I.*

*Left: Bradham and the Pepsi-Cola Company actively supported the war. Bradham gave speeches urging the American people to conserve natural resources to ensure that the nation's troops would be adequately supplied.*

that would eventually play a role in the bankruptcy of Pepsi-Cola.

With the start of World War I, four of the world's leading sugar producers were in opposition. An area of central Europe considered one of the prime agricultural zones for beet sugar was under attack. As a result, the market was short an estimated one million pounds of sugar a month. Furthermore, off fighting the war was the labor supply that harvested the crop, and included among the war's casualties were sugar refineries. Consequently, the world sugar supply dropped sharply.

The United States may have obtained the bulk of its sugar from cane grown in Cuba, but much of this source was being diverted to help offset the loss of central Europe's sugar crop. Sugar dealers quickly took advantage of the situation: Within two months of the start of the war, the price of sugar jumped to seven cents per pound—twice the cost of several months earlier.

Because sugar is not only the largest single ingredient but also the most expensive item in the recipe for Pepsi-Cola syrup, the rising price of sugar halted any further expansion of the Pepsi-Cola Company. The increase of just three and a half cents a pound upped the cost of producing syrup by 25 cents a gallon. Given that the license agreement signed by the bottlers and the parent company fixed the price of syrup at $1.25 a gallon, the increased cost for sugar would have to be absorbed somehow by one or both parties. It was well understood that charging more than a nickel for a bottle of Pepsi-Cola would drastically cut sales.

Consumers were convinced that a soft drink should cost only five cents,

*Despite the instability of*

*the sugar market, Pepsi-*

*Cola continued their*

*advertising programs.*

*Many ads run in local*

*newspapers were paid*

*for by the local bottler,*

*with the Pepsi-Cola*

*Company offering the*

*bottler a rebate.*

and any company that dared to charge more risked damage to its public image. Competitors who sold inferior soft drinks certainly wouldn't raise their prices. Consequently, due to a dramatic loss in profits, it became unfeasible for Pepsi-Cola to simultaneously maintain its quality, continue to advertise, and support bottle cap redemption programs.

Nevertheless, Bradham determined that Pepsi-Cola would continue to be promoted. "I intend to place Pepsi-Cola in every home in the United States during the course of the next few years," he stated. His reasoning was that increased sales could offset the decreased profit margin owing to sugar's inflated pricing. Therefore, at the beginning of 1917, Pepsi-Cola launched one of its most ambitious and innovative promotions.

The house-to-house strategy developed by H. Gamse & Brother Lithographers of Baltimore, Maryland, was directed at housewives. Young ladies would appear at the door with samples in the hopes of a sale. Notably, to recruit their workforce, the Gamse Company ran HELP WANTED ads in various newspapers, claiming that becoming a Pepsi girl could improve one's life. Not surprisingly, wherever it was conducted, the campaign never failed to draw attention.

Meanwhile, because the cost of sugar was constantly changing, it was very difficult to work out a pricing structure. The erratic supply of sugar resulted in some bottlers not receiving syrup in time for bottling. Ads run during this period were a waste of money as they enticed the

*As the sugar*

*crisis grew worse,*

*many promotions*

*and incentives were*

*discontinued, including*

*coupons for a free Pepsi.*

# fire horses "whicker" for pepsi-cola

What would make two inhabitants of the High Point, North Carolina, Fire Department habitual drinkers of Pepsi-Cola? Why, horse sense, trumpeted the Southern Carbonator and Bottler magazine in 1916. Apparently, besides "smashing speed records in going to fires or frisking along streets taking a 'constitutional,'" fire horses Duke and Joe had developed the habit of imbibing the soft drink.

"Not a day goes by but they are given a bottle or two of this great American beverage," stated the periodical. Just how the two became enamored of Pepsi was not clear. Noted, however, was the proximity of the Pepsi-Cola bottling plant to fire station No. 1.

Citing the local High Point Enterprise, the Southern Carbonator and Bottler reported this telling behavior: "They [the horses] will raise their heads when they see the bottles [of Pepsi-Cola] approaching, and then with an anticipatory half-closing of the eyes, denoting joy, will tilt back their heads in true human position and still more like a human, let the liquid gurgle down their throats." Moreover, Duke and Joe were said to recognize the "pop" resulting from the removal of the bottle cap by "immediately" emitting a "pleading whicker." The Enterprise went on to claim: "After every trip to a fire the first thing they look for upon returning to the fire station is a bottle of Pepsi-Cola each" and, happily, they "are not disappointed."

customer to crave a product that simply wasn't available. This hurt Pepsi's effort to build a loyal customer base.

The crisis deepened when the United States entered the war in 1917. Some of the raw materials used to produce Pepsi-Cola, such as the tin in bottle caps, were diverted for war use. Almost overnight there were shortages of everything. To make matters worse, a war tax of five cents a gallon was levied on Pepsi-Cola syrup. Some bottlers, unable to absorb the price increase, began diluting the syrup in an effort to produce more than the standard 144 bottles from a gallon of the stuff. Unfortunately, adulterating the syrup changed the taste, which caused an alarming drop in sales.

To stave off diminishing profits and ensure bottlers an adequate supply of Pepsi-Cola syrup, Bradham was determined to find a sugar substitute. Consequently, he investigated the use of saccharin, an artificial sweetener. However, because many states prohibited the use of saccharin, if Bradham had any hopes in this sugar substitute, the law would have to be changed. He wrote articles for trade magazines and lobbied state agencies to no avail. For the time being, saccharin was not the answer to Pepsi-Cola's problems. The Department of Agriculture even stepped in to develop a formula to use less sugar in soft drinks, with disappointing results.

Inconsistent supplies of sugar, fluctuating prices, and an inability to deliver Pepsi-Cola to customers were taking a toll on the parent company and bottlers alike, ruining Pepsi-Cola's thus-far sterling reputation. Bradham's dream was beginning to slip away.

—to the last drop!

YES, sir!—you want it *all*—every teeny-weeny drop For, you know, a single sip of this sparkling, jumping joy-o'-life makes you want *all you can get* of the big nickel's worth.

Be your own judge! There is no substitute for PEPSI-Cola—resent the suggestion.

First for the kiddies, too—get from the grocer a crate for your ice-box. Or at all founts

DRINK **PEPSI-Cola** for Healthful Refreshment

*Ads for Pepsi-Cola sought to convince the consumer of the distinctiveness of Pepsi-Cola.*

Yet, despite the damage to his business brought on by the war, Bradham never complained, believing that to do so would be unpatriotic. In fact, he sponsored Liberty Bond rallies at Pepsi's bottling plants. He also encouraged employees eligible for the draft to volunteer for service.

Expansion, of course, was out of the question. Barely enough syrup was available for bottlers to produce at prewar levels. The Pepsi-Cola Company was trying desperately to satisfy current bottler demands. All that was left for the parent company as well as the bottlers was to try to survive, confident that once the situation returned to normal, they could again figure prominently in the soft drink industry.

Bradham himself remained optimistic. In a letter dated April 28, 1917, he mentioned a plan to increase capital stock to $2 million. He predicted that Prohibition, still a few years in the future, in banning alcoholic beverages throughout the country, would allow for the extension of business to every corner of the country. The soft drink industry could offer an alternative, legal refreshment to a thirsty public. Although he scaled down his planning due to the war, he never gave it up entirely. One of his wartime proposals was to build a syrup plant in Omaha or Kansas City to facilitate what he anticipated would be an inevitable expansion.

Toward the end of 1917, the sugar situation had become so severe that the government ordered restrictions on its sale. At the same time, Congress was moved to investigate whether or not the sugar shortage was artificially induced. It was suspected that sugar-hoarding speculators started a rumor of sugar scarcity, which caused panic buying by the public. Because so much sugar was being shipped to the Allies in Europe, it was relatively easy to fuel this panic in order to drive up the price. Congressional probes, however, failed to result in any prosecutions.

By May 1918, sugar was being rationed to various large users, including soft drink bottlers. In September, the government imposed price controls, setting the price of sugar at nine cents a pound. The sugar used in producing Pepsi-Cola syrup thus cost three times what it had before the start of the war. This amounted to Pepsi-Cola syrup being priced at $1.25 a gallon, containing as it did 59 cents' worth of sugar. As a result, Pepsi-Cola was either breaking even or losing money.

On November 11, 1918, the armistice bringing World War I to an end was signed. Bradham hoped this would also bring to an end his sugar dilemma. This was not to be. Rail strikes and high demand continued to cause instability in the sugar market, keeping prices high and supply low.

In the fall of 1919, Pepsi-Cola was advised that they would receive the same quantity of sugar for October, November, and December that they had received for the same period the year before. Pepsi-Cola encouraged their bottlers to focus on filling orders for their regular customers. Even such conservation measures didn't help. By late 1919, the Pepsi-Cola Company lacked the sugar to produce their syrup.

The consequences were felt throughout the Pepsi bottler network. Many bottlers had to shut down, having nothing to bottle

and nothing to deliver. It wasn't until the end of 1919 that Bradham was able to buy the necessary sugar at 18 cents a pound, producing syrup that would cost $1.60 a gallon.

During the last few years of the war, the ever-resourceful Bradham had bought sugar from any available source. One supplier had sold Bradham sugar that had been mixed with molasses. Once the Pepsi-Cola produced from this sugar reached the market, however, consumers complained about its taste. Although the tainted syrup fortunately was not distributed to all the Pepsi bottlers, those who did use it suffered lost sales and a further deterioration of their product's reputation.

Concerned about declining sales, a few of the affected bottlers suggested adding a stimulant to Pepsi-Cola. Bradham understood they were referring to caffeine, an additive Pepsi had tested in the past. Although Bradham had always been proud that Pepsi-Cola was considered pure and safe even for children to drink, by 1919 sales had declined so severely that he was willing to acquiesce to the bottlers' demand. He agreed to add caffeine to the syrup for those bottlers who requested it.

The beginning of the new year, 1920, offered hope for the Pepsi-Cola Company. Now that the sugar crisis would be soon behind them, they had faith that they would be shipping regular supplies of syrup to their bottlers. Thanks to this optimism, the Pepsi-Cola Company crafted their most aggressive advertising program since the war years. The theme was DRINK PEPSI-COLA—IT WILL SATISFY YOU. For the first time, Pepsi screened commercials in movie theaters.

A monopoly in the sugar trade, however, undermined the campaign. The expected normalization of sugar prices and supplies was thwarted by a cartel of Cuban

*Many of the more successful Pepsi-Cola bottlers were able to keep their businesses operating through the sugar crises and Pepsi-Cola's bankruptcy.*

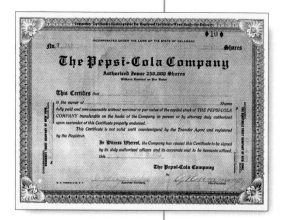

*In 1922, Bradham, with the help of R.C. Megargel, started a new Pepsi-Cola Company complete with new stock. Only a few shares were ever sold.*

sugar growers. Under the guise of stabilizing sugar prices, farmers and distributors had formed an organization aimed at manipulating sugar merchants. The efforts of this group slowed the release of their product, causing demand to exceed supply. Panic buying promptly drove prices up. In March, the price of sugar was 9.5 cents per pound; in April, the price rose to 13.75 cents per pound; by May it had reached 27 cents per pound. Anxious about future price and availability, Pepsi-Cola bought 10,000 pounds of this 27-cent sugar, causing the price of syrup to shoot up to $2.32 per gallon.

Pepsi-Cola was not the only soft drink hit hard by the turbulent sugar market of 1920. Coca-Cola would lose $2 million as a result of fluctuating sugar prices.

Some attribute Bradham's financial ruin to the inflation of sugar pricing. Examining the numbers, one can see that even if Pepsi had sold their syrup at $1.25 a gallon, resulting in a loss of just over $1,700, that amount should have been negligible to the company. Multiply that figure by 10 to make the loss $17,000, and it still wouldn't have been enough to devastate Pepsi's fortunes. But that loss, added to several years of losses and combined with a decline in sales brought on by the sugar crisis, may have been enough to wreck Bradham's dreams for Pepsi-Cola.

The beginning of 1921 found the Pepsi-Cola Company completely broke. Needing immediate cash, Bradham took out a mortgage on the Pepsi-Cola building for $60,000 with the Dixie Fire Insurance Co. The hemorrhage of money continued. Bradham needed serious financial help and fast. He turned to the New York firm of R.C. Megargel and Company. Megargel suggested a reorganization plan that involved a new company to be registered in Delaware. The plan was to raise sufficient capital through stock sales to pay off the debt and have enough left over to expand the business. An expansion could produce the needed revenue to make this a lucrative proposition for all concerned.

On February 20, 1922, the new Pepsi-Cola Company was incorporated in Wilmington, Delaware, with Megargel named as a director. Once again, Caleb Bradham was president. New York City was listed as the company's headquarters, and the nature of its business was stated to be holding stock of the Pepsi-Cola Company, a North Carolina corporation.

Megargel made a valiant effort to find investors for the company. He printed brochures recounting the history of Pepsi-Cola and projected healthy revenues for the next four years. Unable to find enough investors, however, the company failed to pull themselves out of debt. The end came for Bradham and the New Bern era of Pepsi-Cola on May 31, 1923, when the company was certified bankrupt.

Pepsi-Cola had begun its second decade with assets of $100,000 over liabilities. Alarmingly, 13 years later, their liabilities exceeded their assets by more than $56,000. What this added up to was disaster. And, with the majority of Pepsi-Cola's assets tied up in real estate, there was no way to turn the business around quickly.

On May 7, 1923, the assets of the Pepsi-Cola Company were bought up by the Craven Holding Corporation.

# the story of the "pepsi girl"

BEFORE I BECAME A
Pepsi-Cola Girl

Did you ever work in a department store? I tried it for several years and a pretty looking wreck it made of me. I read the HELP WANTED columns and found an ad that interested me. They wanted me to demonstrate a soft drink that I had never even heard of—Pepsi-Cola!

As the train pulled out of Baltimore, I was scared green, not knowing what I was getting into. When it reached New Bern, the sun was shining bright, so I couldn't help being a little cheered up.

I was surprised when I got inside the building. Everything was spotlessly clean, and Pepsi-Cola rose in my estimation right away. Mr. Bradham, the President, treated me like I was a real person, not a machine. He saw that I was given some Pepsi to drink. It was grand!

The morning I started out I realized it was going to be easy for me to sell Pepsi-Cola because I believed in it. The combination of lovely Southern people, Pepsi-Cola, fresh air, and exercise have turned me into a new being and I love my work.

As Mamie over at the ribbon counter would say, "Believe me, this is the life!"

---

The "Pepsi Girl" before and after.

AFTER I BECAME A
PEPSI-COLA GIRL

# RICHMOND

## VIRGINIA

APRIL, 1929

15c Per Copy. $1.50 Per Year.

THE NATIONAL PEPSI-COLA CORPORATION, 1224 WEST BROAD STREET
"THE HOME OF PEPSI-COLA"

Published by RICHMOND CHAMBER OF COMMERCE, MASON MANGHUM, *Managing Director*

# here's health

As the year 1923 dawned, Thomas S. Southgate of Norfolk, Virginia, the largest unsecured creditor of the Pepsi-Cola Company, surveyed the future of the company and found it far from rosy. Consequently, on January 30, he organized the Craven Holding Corporation.

The corporation's bylaws commissioned it to manufacture, buy, sell, and deal in nonintoxicating beverages of all kinds and descriptions. Additionally, the company purposed to subscribe, to purchase or otherwise acquire, and to guarantee or become surety in respect to the stock, bonds, or other securities and obligations of other companies. In other words, the Craven Holding Corporation had been set up to buy out other creditors for the purpose of taking control of the Pepsi-Cola formula and trademark. Some creditors were indeed bought out, while others were appeased with shares in the newly formed corporation.

Eventually, the Craven Holding Corporation achieved its intention to be in position to buy the assets, real estate, and personal property of the Pepsi-Cola Company. As if on cue, on April 17, 1923, the court ordered trustee R.B. Williams to sell the assets of the Pepsi-Cola Company to the Craven Holding Corporation. The price: $35,000— half in cash and half in a promissory note due in six months.

The Craven Holding Corporation now held Pepsi-Cola's two most important assets: its formula and trademark. The formula was mysteriously locked in a safe-deposit box by court order, with specific instructions disallowing anyone to view it. This secrecy held until July 1923, when the bankruptcy court finally granted the trustees permission to release the formula to the Craven Holding Corporation.

Together, the formula and the trademark were duly transferred to the Pepsi-Cola Corporation of Richmond, Virginia,

*The five-story building located at 1224 West Broad Street, Richmond, Virginia, home to Taka-Kola, became the new home of Pepsi-Cola in July 1923.*

*Although the trademark and formula would change hands with the bankruptcy, it was the franchise Pepsi-Cola bottlers who made sure the soft drink was continuously available.*

in exchange for stock in the corporation. This gave the Craven Holding Corporation what they wanted all along—a continued interest in Pepsi-Cola. Pepsi-Cola promptly began production and distribution from its new home: 1224 West Broad Street, Richmond, Virginia.

While the Pepsi-Cola bankruptcy was being resolved in New Bern, a new com-

pany became incorporated hundreds of miles away in Richmond. The Pepsi-Cola Corporation, established June 15, 1923, was born of a merger between the Craven Holding Corporation, holder of the Pepsi-Cola trademark and formula, and the Old Dominion Beverage Company, owner of a soft drink manufacturing plant in Richmond, headed by Clyde W. Saunders.

Old Dominion's choice of the name Taka-Kola was a deliberate scheme to confuse consumers; that is, customers expecting Coca-Cola were being tricked into buying Taka-Kola. Unscrupulous fountain retailers were suspected of mixing Taka-Kola and Coca-Cola and serving the Coca-Cola customer a compromised product. The charge of substitution applied when a customer who intended to buy Coca-Cola entered a grocery store that offered other cola drinks. In sum, the consumer who purchased anything but Coca-Cola was not simply exercising choice but was instead a victim of fraud. Presenting such arguments was nothing new for the Coca-Cola Company, having made equivalent claims in lawsuits against other competitors.

Not surprisingly, Coca-Cola sued Old Dominion Beverage in court. As a result, Taka-Kola was slapped with a ruling accusing it of violating Coca-Cola's trademark.

Old Dominion Beverage promptly changed the name of their product to Takola. Unimpressed by this gesture, Coca-Cola again sued Old Dominion for trademark infringement. And again, Old Dominion was restricted by the U.S. District Court from using their product name.

What Old Dominion Beverage desperately needed was a cola drink that would protect it from trademark infringement lawsuits by Coca-Cola. Meanwhile, in New Bern, the financially strapped Pepsi-Cola Company stood ready to fill that need. Their trademark, in circulation for over 20 years, had never been challenged by Coca-Cola. In fact, the Pepsi-Cola trademark was as well established as Coca-Cola's. As a bonus, they had a large following of loyal customers in Old Dominion territory.

*In an effort to promote and reinforce the image of Pepsi-Cola, some bottlers began using a standardized bottle. However, without the support of the parent company behind it, this bottle never caught on.*

Old Dominion had been incorporated in 1903 to manufacture, bottle, and distribute carbonated drinks. At a later date, they began producing and selling a cola drink known as Taka-Kola. The increasing popularity of this beverage invariably caught the attention of the Coca-Cola Company in Atlanta, Georgia.

Coca-Cola became convinced that

Like a Million Dollars and a Happy Disposition

# Pepsi-Cola

BOOSTS AND CHEERS

*Pepifying—with fruity flavors appealing to taste*

"YOUR VERDICT"

SO MUCH BETTER—MADE IN RICHMOND

*By*

## Pepsi-Cola Corporation

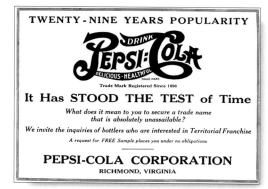

TWENTY-NINE YEARS POPULARITY

DRINK Pepsi-Cola

DELICIOUS—HEALTHFUL TRADE MARK

Trade Mark Registered Since 1896

It Has STOOD THE TEST of Time

*What does it mean to you to secure a trade name
that is absolutely unassailable?*

*We invite the inquiries of bottlers who are interested in Territorial Franchise*

*A request for FREE Sample places you under no obligations*

**PEPSI-COLA CORPORATION**

RICHMOND, VIRGINIA

Despite bankruptcy, from February until June 1923, Pepsi-Cola syrup was still being produced and sold. This met with the approval of court and creditors, fully aware that ceasing production of Pepsi-Cola would pass a death sentence onto the value of the trademark. Pepsi-Cola's creditors, anxious to recoup their losses from the trademark's sale, thus had an interest in its continued viability. Meanwhile, the efforts taken to keep the Pepsi-Cola trademark alive indicates how the company's many years of advertising had infused the name with value.

In April 1923, trustee R.B. Williams took an extraordinary step. He drafted a letter of support for the new Pepsi-Cola Corporation that he then sent to the remaining Pepsi-Cola bottlers. Under normal circumstances, the trustee works for the court to protect the interest of the creditors, but in this case, Williams was clearly promoting the Pepsi-Cola Corporation of Richmond, Virginia. The letter hinted at his motivation with a mention that following his duties as trustee, he could be contacted at the offices of the Pepsi-Cola Corporation.

Written on stationery from the Pepsi-Cola Company of New Bern, the letter formally announced to bottlers the transfer of name, trademark, and formula to the Pepsi-Cola Corporation of Richmond, Virginia. Additionally, it mentioned plans for an upcoming Pepsi-Cola bottlers convention to be held in August.

The convention was geared toward reassuring bottlers of the Pepsi-Cola Corporation's commitment to stand behind every gallon of syrup they produced. The bottlers, for their part, were invited to present wish lists in the way of advertising.

Although the Pepsi-Cola Corporation of Richmond, Virginia, functioned as a continuation of the original Pepsi-Cola Company, few involved with Pepsi-Cola of New Bern made the move to Richmond. One who did was Roy C. Megargel, buying shares in both the Craven Holding Corporation and the Pepsi-Cola Corporation. One can only guess why Megargel remained on board an apparently sinking ship. Perhaps he, like Caleb Bradham, fell in love with the dream of making Pepsi-Cola a world-famous soft drink. In any case, he devoted considerable time and money to making Pepsi-Cola successful.

At the time of incorporation, Megargel was listed as the president of the Pepsi-Cola Corporation. In hopes the stock would quickly be redeemed, thus giving Megargel complete control of the company, Old Dominion stockholders were traded preferred stock in Pepsi-Cola. Yet, for reasons known only to themselves, those stock-holders handed Clyde W. Saunders the presidency of the Pepsi-Cola Corporation, relegating Megargel, despite his holding a majority of the stock, to a seat on the board of directors. One can only guess that they discounted Megargel's active involvement as he divided his time between his company in New York and the Pepsi-Cola Corporation in Richmond.

By 1923, the much-anticipated postwar economic expansion was going gang-busters. Many businesses, including the soft drink industry, benefited from the giddy consumerism of the Roaring '20s.

Additionally, with Prohibition the law of the land since 1920, more and more people were contenting themselves with carbonated beverages. Ushered in with the passage of the 18th Amendment to the Constitution, the period known as Prohibition barred Americans from the manufacture, sale, transport, import, export, delivery, furnishing, or possession of any intoxicating liquor—except for medicinal purposes in, of all places, drugstores. Lasting until the abrogation of the amendment in 1933, the so-called Noble Experiment outlawed liquor, beer, and wine throughout the land.

In the midst of America's economic prosperity and with increasing demand for their product, the Pepsi-Cola Corporation nevertheless found itself in the unenviable position of starting over almost from scratch. Pepsi's bottling network and fountain syrup distributing system practically had to be rebuilt.

The Pepsi-Cola Corporation numbered the bottling agents actively producing Pepsi-Cola in 1923 at 70. Even if that amount were correct, only a small percent did much volume. During the sugar crises

*Roy C. Megargel was enlisted by Bradham to help rescue Pepsi-Cola from debt. Failing to raise enough capital to accomplish this feat, Megargel, caught up in the excitement of the business, nevertheless became an investor. He remained a financial supporter of the company until the 1931 bankruptcy.*

of the New Bern era, many had simply gone out of business. Others had canceled their licensing agreements with Pepsi-Cola to enable them to service other cola manufacturers. The remaining bottlers faced enormous obstacles in restoring public confidence in the quality of Pepsi-Cola. Above all, trust had to be reestablished with retailers not only to persuade them to stock the product but also to enlist their aid in promoting it.

Consequently, rebuilding the bottler network became the number one priority for the new Pepsi-Cola Corporation. The board figured the only way to achieve success was to expand beyond the southeastern United States, which had embraced Pepsi-Cola as a local drink. The goal of the Pepsi-Cola Corporation—as had been Bradham's—was to serve the entire country from coast to coast.

To attract new bottlers, the Pepsi-Cola Corporation placed enticing ads in various bottler magazines, offering free samples of Pepsi-Cola with no strings attached. The ads made a point of claiming their trademark was unassailable, clearly referring to Coca-Cola's inability to annihilate Pepsi-Cola on the basis of trademark infringement. They also credited Pepsi-Cola with standing the test of time, mistakenly placing Pepsi-Cola's start, however, in 1896.

Meanwhile, studiously applying what they had learned from the New Bern bankruptcy about the instability of the sugar market, the Pepsi-Cola Corporation sold their syrup in concentrate rather than in the traditional finished form. A finished syrup is complete and ready to use, whereas a syrup concentrate needs first to be mixed with other ingredients, usually water and sugar.

**And to whet the appetite—Pepsi-Cola!**

To make you really enjoy your meals on days when you "just don't care whether school keeps or not," there is no more effective and satisfying help than a cold glass of Pepsi-Cola.

The real thirst-quencher—combines refreshment with a bracing effect that does away with the discomforts of heat and fatigue.

**PEPSI·Cola**

Served at all fountains — also at your grocer's, carbonated in bottles.

*For All Thirsts ·Pepsi-Cola*

Thus, Pepsi-Cola avoided having to buy large quantities of sugar and adjust the price of their syrup based on the fluctuating cost of sugar. This strategy, of course, put the burden of acquiring sugar on the bottlers. But it also reduced the weight of the syrup, helping to keep costs down.

The early years in Richmond were bereft of print advertising. Eventually, following the recruitment of a local advertising firm, a series of ads was created specifically for newspapers and magazines. The Richmond Pepsi-Cola Corporation also launched a bottle cap redemption program similar to that introduced by the New Bern company.

All in all, the amount of advertising done was far too little to transform Pepsi-Cola into a major cola company. Instead, they remained only one of many in competition to become America's number-two cola behind Coca-Cola. Among the contenders were Chero-Cola, Vera-Cola, Afri-Kola, and Celery-Cola.

Local bottlers generated some advertising, but without a common theme and well-orchestrated approach, their combined efforts lacked impact. For one thing, while all bottles of this period were sized at six to seven ounces and sealed with an orange-and-black cap, Pepsi-Cola failed to endorse a standard glass container. Although some bottlers promoted a bottle with a distinctive design, it never became widely used.

By 1928, it became apparent that the Pepsi-Cola Corporation had made embarrassingly little progress. Forced to virtually start over in Richmond, they had fallen far short of reaching the level of success enjoyed by Pepsi-Cola New Bern in its early days.

It became painfully evident, too, that Pepsi-Cola Corporation's finances, teetering

*Above left: Pepsi-Cola ads were designed to attract consumers by offering a combination of refreshment and health benefits.*

*Above right: Many Pepsi-Cola bottlers bottled other soft drinks. Usually these offered an assortment of flavors, including such fruit tastes as orange and grape.*

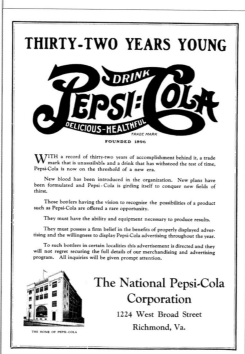

## THIRTY-TWO YEARS YOUNG

WITH a record of thirty-two years of accomplishment behind it, a trade mark that is unassailable and a drink that has withstood the test of time, Pepsi-Cola is now on the threshold of a new era.

New blood has been introduced in the organization. New plans have been formulated and Pepsi-Cola is girding itself to conquer new fields of thirst.

Those bottlers having the vision to recognize the possibilities of a product such as Pepsi-Cola are offered a rare opportunity.

They must have the ability and equipment necessary to produce results.

They must possess a firm belief in the benefits of properly displayed advertising and the willingness to display Pepsi-Cola advertising throughout the year.

To such bottlers in certain localities this advertisement is directed and they will not regret securing the full details of our merchandising and advertising program. All inquiries will be given prompt attention.

**The National Pepsi-Cola Corporation**

1224 West Broad Street
Richmond, Va.

THE HOME OF PEPSI-COLA

on crisis, had only worsened following the agreement joining them to the Old Dominion Beverage Company. The year 1925 had heralded the alarming fact that the Old Dominion stockholder's preferred stock in the Pepsi-Cola Corporation was past due for redemption. This, plus the pressure of dividend payments owed Old Dominion stockholders, pushed the Pepsi-Cola Corporation toward financial disaster.

To prevent the impending crisis, another corporation was formed. On August 23, 1928, the Pepsi-Cola Corporation of Richmond, Virginia, merged with a brand-new Pepsi-Cola Company—the National Pepsi-Cola Corporation, also of Richmond. The National Pepsi-Cola Corporation had been incorporated a mere matter of weeks earlier, on July 31, 1928. The joint resolution merging the two companies called for a rehaul of the terms and conditions of the Pepsi-Cola Corporation's charter as to the holding of stock as well as for a plan to refinance and reorganize the business to ensure its survival.

### A Moving Billboard---A Bright, Snappy, Green Truck---Keep 'em Clean

Paint your truck standard *Pepsi-Cola* green all over—

Letter Pepsi-Cola trade marks large and prominent in white outlined in black . . . The words "Drink," "Here's Health," "Try," "You'll like it," "Bottling Company" and your address should be lettered in red with a yellow outline . . . Follow blue print to reproduce the Pepsi-Cola trade mark absolutely accurately.

The above illustration gives you a good general layout to follow . . . Paint all your trucks in this snappy style . . . It pays to dress up your delivery equipment . . . A downtown bulletin is valuable advertising but quite expensive . . . Your trucks are in the heart of town daily . . . It pays to advertise!

A clean truck speaks for a clean, sanitary plant and represents quality merchandise . . . A clean truck will impress the dealer, the dealer will do business with a live progressive organization . . . A clean truck will back up your salesmen on every route . . . All aggressive bottlers keep their trucks clean.

A rivalry had raged between Megargel and the Old Dominion stockholders from the Pepsi-Cola Corporation's very start. Now, the hope was that somehow a brand-new corporation with a brand-new management team could unite the fragmented company.

Oddly, Roy Megargel and Clyde Saunders, the two individuals most responsible for Pepsi-Cola's reemergence in Virginia, were nothing more than stockholders in the National Pepsi-Cola Corporation. The new board of directors consisted of three lawyers: R. Carter Scott Jr., Robert E. Scott, and Holt S. Lloyd, who also served as officers of the corporation, with R. Carter Scott Jr. acting as president.

Why the stockholders chose lawyers to oversee the new corporation remains a mystery. Perhaps this arrangement was the product of compromise between the two warring groups of stockholders. In any case, while the current board helped to stabilize the corporation, for sustained, long-term growth, Pepsi-Cola would need management conversant with the intricacies of the soft drink industry.

The soft drink industry was still a fledgling enterprise, and many practices and procedures flew by trial and error. The ideal leaders of the Pepsi-Cola Corporation would have been experienced in the ins and outs of the industry. They would have been knowledgeable about how to sell Pepsi-Cola and about how to motivate the bottlers to do the same.

Be that as it may, the National Pepsi-Cola Corporation's new management took over in November 1928. The tasks they faced included polishing up Pepsi-Cola's image and recruiting bottlers.

First off, a new advertising slogan was unveiled: HERE'S HEALTH, with the tag line TRY PEPSI—YOU'LL LIKE IT. In addition, a bright, snappy green was designated the signature color for promoting the soft drink.

To ensure uniformity, bottlers were supplied with brochures showing precisely how to transform their truck into a moving billboard. Paint your truck standard Pepsi-Cola green all over, it exhorted. It also directed that the Pepsi-Cola trademark be prominently displayed in white outlined in black and that the new slogan—emblazoned on the back and sides—be lettered in red with a yellow outline.

*In their most concerted effort for uniformity thus far, Pepsi-Cola directed bottlers to use their new official bottle. Unfortunately, this innovation came too late to make a difference.*

*The official bottle of the Pepsi-Cola Corporation, introduced in July 1929, held 6.5 ounces and was topped with a green-and-white cap.*

To further cue the public to the distinctiveness of their product, in July 1929 the company introduced their first standard Pepsi-Cola bottle. Holding six ounces, then considered to be a full serving, this bottle sported the trademark name embossed in the glass. So singular was the design that it was patented.

The task of amassing new bottlers had begun in earnest at the American Bottlers of Carbonated Beverages Convention in January 1929. Soft drink bottlers from all over the United States flocked to the convention site, providing an excellent opportunity to sign them to Pepsi-Cola. Indeed, whole new territories opened up to the company, and for the very first time, a Pepsi-Cola bottler set up shop in the enemy camp, serving Atlanta, Georgia, hometown of Coca-Cola.

The National Pepsi-Cola Corporation was finally on track, moving toward their goal of becoming a national soft drink company. Then, once again, circumstances beyond their control intervened. On October 29, 1929, the U.S. stock market crashed. Between 1929 and

poration then owed Megargel $50,603.91, not including the losses from the Pepsi-Cola stock he owned.

As Pepsi-Cola faced bankruptcy, once again, a candy store chain in New York was battling Coca-Cola, their supplier of fountain syrup. Many of Loft Candies' 138 stores featured soda fountains, whose combined operation required nearly 100 gallons of cola syrup daily.

Questioning the adequacy of their discount for such a large volume, Loft's president, Charles Guth, called a meeting with a representative from Coca-Cola. Coca-Cola, however, refused to up the discount, prompting Guth to issue a memo to his staff, inquiring, "Why are you paying the full price for Coca-Cola? Can you handle this, or would you suggest our buying Pepsi-Cola at about $1 per gallon?" No one is quite sure whether Guth intended this as a bluff to eventually persuade Coca-Cola to lower their price. In any case, the memo was dated May 19, 1931, just one day after a Pepsi-Cola enterprise was again forced into bankruptcy.

The crash of the stock market had nearly obliterated the fortunes of Pepsi-Cola. Following their bankruptcy, they, their creditors, and one Horace H. Edwards, the court-appointed trustee, agreed it would be in the best interest of all parties for the National Pepsi-Cola Corporation to continue to operate—under Edward's watchful eye—in hopes that the entire property could be sold as a whole.

Meanwhile, a significant error inexplicably occurred in the appraisal of the corporation's assets, estimating them all—including formula, trademark, and patent—to be worth a single value of $10,950. At the same time, an auction was arranged to sell off these assets, along with other property

1931, an estimated $50 billion was lost on Wall Street, ushering in a devastating period in American history known as the Great Depression. Massive unemployment signaled the average American's alarming lack of income—disposable or otherwise.

The National Pepsi-Cola Corporation managed to survive through 1930, but in May 1931 their creditors forced them into involuntary bankruptcy. Megargel, who had reached into his own pocket so many times to keep Pepsi solvent, could no longer afford to do so. Their bankruptcy records, meanwhile, reveal that the Pepsi-Cola Cor-

HERE'S HEALTH *was the last*

*slogan used in the Richmond*

*era of Pepsi-Cola history.*

*Loft Candies operated stores*

*throughout the greater New*

*York area. A dispute with*

*Coca-Cola, the original*

*supplier of cola syrup for their*

*soda fountains, brought Loft*

*to Pepsi's aid, pulling it out*

*of bankruptcy.*

of the now-bankrupt National Pepsi-Cola Corporation.

The day before the auction date, Roy Megargel approached Edwards and offered him $9,600 for the formula and trademark. Apparently, Megargel believed this to be enough of a bargain not to take the risk of obtaining them for less at auction.

Edwards, with the estimate of $10,950 for the entire package in mind, was agreeable, but he needed to act quickly. Megargel's offer was good only for that day. Edwards speedily sought, and received, permission from the court to sell before auction.

Megargel's maneuver fueled controversy in subsequent years. In 1939, Alexander W. Herman, a stockholder in the National Pepsi-Cola Corporation, brought a lawsuit against Charles Guth, Megargel, and Pepsi-Cola, accusing them of fraudulently obtaining the trademark from the bankruptcy sale. In his suit, Herman assessed the true value of the trademark and formula at $1,000,000. Although the suit was eventually dismissed, one can't help but wonder what the actual worth of the trademark may have been.

When news of the Pepsi-Cola bankruptcy reached Guth, he immediately contacted Megargel to set up a meeting to discuss the future of Pepsi-Cola. The result was an agreement, signed on July 23, 1931, for Guth to incorporate a new Pepsi-Cola Company. The incorporation itself took place on August 10, 1931.

Although Guth's immediate objective may have been to more economically supply Loft soda fountains with cola, his request for company records and a customer list suggest he had bigger plans. Perhaps Megargel had passed on to Guth a bit of his own unfailing belief in Pepsi-Cola's potential for success. Megargel, after all,

had been the driving force behind Pepsi-Cola's continued existence following the New Bern bankruptcy.

In any event, the agreement stated that Guth would organize a corporation known as the Pepsi-Cola Company of New York and employ the trademark and formula owned by Megargel. In exchange, Megargel was to be paid $25,000 a year for the next six years—or $150,000 total. Additionally, he was to receive 2.5 cents royalty on every gallon of Pepsi-Cola sold as well as one third of the issued stock. Although Megargel may not have gotten much cash up front, the terms of this agreement had the potential to pay millions. Just by itself, $150,000 would be worth well over $1 million in today's market.

Because Megargel had developed friendships with bottlers going back to the New Bern days, he intended the agreement with Guth to protect bottlers currently under contract with Pepsi-Cola. Guth agreed only in spirit, making sure to insert an escape clause denying the company's obligation to abide by those contracts. Thus, early on, Guth signaled his desire to be in total control of Pepsi-Cola.

*In the 1940s and 1950s, the Pepsi-Cola crown, also known as a bottle cap, would become the emblem of the company. However, a coupon from 1929 reveals an early attempt to make the bottle cap the recognized symbol of Pepsi-Cola.*

# "twice as much for a nickel"

**H**appiness, the sign read outside one of the Loft retail stores in the New York area (the names of the other two were Mirror and, simply, Loft). A model of vertical integration, candy manufacturer Loft Incorporated served as their own distributor and retailer, selling their product through a chain of stores. Eager to expand the modest empire, Loft acquired Mavis Candies Incorporated from Charles Guth in July 1929.

In return, Guth received 50,692 shares of Loft Incorporated stock as well as a place on their board of directors. Within eight months, Guth had rallied enough support to oust the other members of the board and replace them with directors loyal to him. The new board quickly installed Guth as president of Loft Inc.

Unluckily for Guth, the coup handing control to him took place just months after the stock market crash. As the nation plunged into the Great Depression, Loft Inc. faced an alarming decline in sales.

Despite more pressing problems, Guth stubbornly latched on to the issue of the cost of Coca-Cola syrup used at Loft soda fountains. Guth contended that based on the volume of syrup used, Loft Inc. should be given wholesale pricing—an argument that left Coca-Cola unimpressed. At this point, most retailers would have either accepted the offered price or switched to a viable competitor. But not Guth—he went out and bought his own cola company.

One has to wonder whether Guth's challenge to Coca-Cola was fueled by a desire for revenge. A few years earlier, Guth had developed Mavis Chocolate Drink, and to ensure distribution of his new beverage, he employed several established bottlers, two of whom serviced Coca-Cola. Within a matter of weeks, sales for Mavis were soaring.

*In 1935, the Pepsi-Cola Bottling Company of California became one of the first company-owned plants outside the New York area. After the 1939 settlement with Guth, this plant was awarded to his sons.*

On September 26, 1931,
a little over a month
after the bankruptcy,
Pepsi-Cola made its
debut in New York City
at the Loft soda fountains.

Charles Guth had been in
the candy manufacturing
business for many years,
but it is his introduction
of Pepsi-Cola in the 12-
ounce bottle for a nickel
for which he is most noted.

Once the Coca-Cola Company discovered that bottlers of Cola-Cola were distributing Mavis Chocolate Drink, however, the bottlers were ordered to cease doing so—immediately. Guth, for his part, was not the type to quit. Overnight, he set up a distributor system for Mavis. Yet, while Mavis continued to operate successfully in Coca-Cola territories, Guth never forgot how he had been treated.

After acquiring the formula for Pepsi-Cola, Guth turned it over to a young chemist employed at the Loft laboratories. Richard J. Ritchie, who would later create a flavor for Pepsi-Cola competitor C & C Cola, made slight adjustments to the Pepsi formula so that the taste was more to Guth's liking. Pepsi-Cola was again primed to enter the cola market.

Confident that he now had a suitable replacement, Guth ordered that henceforth, Coca-Cola would no longer be sold at Loft, Mirror, or Happiness soda fountains. Coca-Cola was taken completely by surprise. In fact, it might be argued that the cola wars began on September 26, 1931, the date Pepsi-Cola replaced Coca-Cola at all Loft stores.

Contrary to Guth's expectations for his new fountain drink, cola sales at Loft outlets began to fall off almost at once. Customers, grown accustomed to Coca-Cola, were reluctant to try a new beverage. Pepsi-Cola had apparently strayed too far from its birthplace in the South for people to recognize its name.

Toward the end of 1931, New York City's Loft laboratories began production of Pepsi-Cola concentrate. In this form, Pepsi-Cola proceeded to a Guth-owned facility in Baltimore operating under the name of the Grace Company, where it was converted into a syrup and distributed to customers,

including Loft Inc. Besides the Loft stores, Pepsi-Cola syrup was sold to a handful of bottlers and to an occasional wholesaler who would resell the syrup to soda fountain operators.

During this period, a handful of Pepsi-Cola bottlers remained in operation. Most notably were the Jessups in Virginia and the Burnetts and Fowlers in North Carolina. While documentation exists that Guth had a representative employed in recruiting more bottlers, there's no evidence of his success. Although the Pepsi-Cola Company did provide bottlers with syrup, bottlers were apparently on their own when it came to advertising.

From 1932 to 1933, the Pepsi-Cola Company was a mere office in New York's Empire State Building. From this tiny center, a negligible sales force ventured forth to enlist bottlers and sell Pepsi-Cola fountain syrup. There is no evidence they had much success.

A letter from S.A. Jessup, the Pepsi-Cola bottler in Charlottesville, to one of his managers in 1932 suggests the company's desperate state during this period. In the letter, Jessup provides instruction in the excruciatingly difficult task of laying off an employee just five days before Christmas.

*Embroiled with Coca-Cola in legal battles, Pepsi's situation was becoming desperate. Some of their few remaining bottlers were on the verge of going out of business.*

*Pepsi-Cola concentrate was produced at the Loft plant in Long Island City, New York, and then sent to Baltimore, Maryland. There it was made into Pepsi-Cola syrup and distributed to bottlers and fountain dispensers.*

To make matters worse, Coca-Cola was accusing the Loft stores of substituting Pepsi-Cola for Coca-Cola without customers' knowledge. The Coca-Cola Company had a way of stretching the definition of *substitution* to suggest that any customer ordering a cola drink expected a Coca-Cola and only a Coca-Cola. As a result, many fountain operators were so intimidated by the threat of being sued that they served Coca-Cola exclusively.

A little over six months after Guth's September 26 directive, Coca-Cola filed a lawsuit against Loft Inc., claiming substitution infringement. The Coca-Cola Company went so far as to petition a Delaware court for a restraining order against Loft Inc. and Happiness Candy Stores Inc. to stop them from serving Pepsi-Cola to patrons requesting Coca-Cola.

A spokesperson for Loft shot back that, in fact, customers requesting Coca-Cola were informed the store did not sell that product, and furthermore, if a customer "accepted Pepsi-Cola and was not satisfied, then his money was refunded." The spokesperson went on to state that "Loft, Inc. serves Pepsi-Cola exclusively because in our opinion, it is superior to any drink of its kind, and in line with our policy of giving to our customers better quality and more for the money. Loft sells an eight-ounce glass of Pepsi-Cola for five cents, in comparison with the average five-ounce drink sold elsewhere."

Taking the offensive, Pepsi-Cola filed a $2 million suit against Coca-Cola. It accused Coca-Cola of interfering with a contract between Pepsi-Cola and Loft. Loft followed with a $5 million suit of their own based on the same claim, compounded with a charge of intimidation against Coca-Cola for attempting to coerce Loft fountains to use them again as suppliers.

Coca-Cola's witnesses at the trial of *Coca-Cola* v. *Loft* included detectives hired to investigate Loft's fountain sales practices. The gumshoes testified to witnessing 620 individual acts of substitution in 44 different Loft and Happiness establishments. Loft Inc. countered that these incidents were created by Coca-Cola hirelings out to trap fountain employees.

**66**

In June 1933, the court ruled against Coca-Cola, concluding that although substitution may have occurred, there was no evidence this was the intent of the Loft management.

To emphasize their commitment to ethical practice, Pepsi-Cola announced they would print a warning on their syrup containers, alerting fountain clerks to the necessity of informing customers they were being served Pepsi-Cola. In a bold publicity move, Loft offered a reward for any customer who could prove that he or she had been a victim of substitution.

Sales of Pepsi-Cola were so abysmally low that by 1933, Guth was entertaining the possibility that he'd made a mistake in acquiring the company. Adding to his headaches, Roy Megargel was complaining he hadn't been paid the money Guth and Pepsi-Cola owed him from the transfer of the trademark. Guth readily expressed his willingness to sell Pepsi-Cola back to Megargel to settle the issue.

Although he declined the offer, Megargel did agree to settle for a reduced amount. Guth next turned to Coca-Cola in hopes they might be interested in buying out their competition. Guth entrusted Loft employee and longtime associate Frank Burns with the delicate task of approaching Coca-Cola with his proposition. Coca-Cola, judging that Pepsi-Cola was on the verge of collapse, turned Guth down. This miscalculation would cost Coca-Cola dearly, forcing them to spend millions of dollars in the coming years to compete with that other cola drink.

Guth figured taking a risk on something new might be just the thing to invigorate Pepsi-Cola's languishing sales. Buying up used 12-ounce beer bottles, he contracted Mavis Bottling to fill the lot with Pepsi-Cola. To gussy the bottles up, they were wrapped with foil around the neck and bottle cap, much like champagne bottles. Priced at 10 cents, this new 12-ounce Pepsi-Cola was sold exclusively through Loft stores.

Unfortunately, the foil-wrapped bottles failed to entice consumers. Sales continued their downward slide. Faced with a growing inventory of 12-ounce Pepsi-Cola bottles, someone decided to reduce the price from 10 cents to a nickel.

The response was astounding. Whether a brilliant marketing idea or a lucky last-ditch effort, with the country in the depths of depression and Pepsi-Cola on the brink of yet another bankruptcy, selling a nickel soft drink was the right move at the right time.

Nevertheless, pragmatist that he was, Guth decided to test-market the innovation outside the New York area to determine its widespread appeal. Baltimore, Maryland, was targeted as the test site. Guth knew a Joe LaPides, who bottled his own line of soft drinks in Baltimore under the name Suburban Club. LaPides had initially worked for Coca-Cola and subsequently sold syrup to soft drink bottlers along the Atlantic seaboard before starting his own bottling business.

In late November 1933, Guth asked LaPides to come to New York. Aware that

*The big five-cent drink*

*is what the 12-ounce*

*Pepsi became in 1934.*

Joe LaVides (back row, third from right) became a territory representative for the Pepsi-Cola Company. In the process of signing up bottlers, he became a close friend to many of them and was affectionately known as Uncle Joe.

whenever Guth summoned someone, it was always important, LaPides replied he would be there the next day. Guth responded that that was not soon enough and suggested he board the next train to New York.

When LaPides arrived at Guth's New York apartment, Guth presented him with the 12-ounce bottle of Pepsi-Cola and explained that when the price was reduced to a nickel, sales went through the roof. True, working on such a narrow margin would be difficult, he continued, but if enough sales were generated, a tidy profit could be made. LaPides was skeptical, but Guth convinced him to try the product in Baltimore, promising to cover any losses. Handed such a guarantee, LaPides could not refuse.

In March 1934, the 12-ounce, five-cent bottle of Pepsi-Cola debuted in Baltimore. The results were almost instantaneous. By May, up to 1,000 cases were being sold in a single day. LaPides wired Guth, advising him of the success of his pricing scheme. Guth was convinced he had a winner. He was now ready to take Pepsi-Cola straight to the top of the soft drink business.

Almost overnight, Pepsi-Cola was forced to change direction: from trying to survive to filling a demand that exceeded their ability to supply. Guth was in desperate need of a bottling plant. In July 1934, he leased the entire production facility at 4751 33rd Street in Long Island City, New York, from the Mavis Bottling Company. Immediately, the building underwent renovation to equip it to produce the wildly popular 12-ounce Pepsi-Cola. In the interim, a makeshift bottling facility was set up at a Loft building in Long Island City.

*Baltimore, Maryland, became the test market for the five-cent 12-ounce bottle of Pepsi. This marked the point where Pepsi-Cola was brought back to life— this time to stay.*

SPARKLING, DELICIOUS!

Almost overnight, Guth's Pepsi-Cola Company went from being a producer of syrup to a bottler of soft drinks. Ensuring capacity to meet demand became Guth's most urgent problem.

Part of Pepsi-Cola's advertising strategy was to remind consumers of the product's long existence. The neck label of the bottle made the claim "Famous for over 30 years." This was naturally confusing to many people who had never heard of Pepsi-Cola.

## Pepsi-Cola

TRADE MARK REG. U.S. PAT. OFF. SINCE 1903

### THE TRUE FACTS

**1.** Pepsi-Cola is absolutely pure, free from preservatives, a combination of more than fifteen of the finest fruit juices, extracts, and other delicious ingredients.

**2.** Pepsi-Cola has been famous for more than 40 years—it is not a new drink. Pepsi-Cola is as stimulating as a fine, fresh cup of tea or coffee—it is *truly* refreshing!

**3.** Pepsi-Cola is distinctly original, not a substitute for any other cola drink, and is a leader in the beverage industry.

**4.** Pepsi-Cola is one of the first bottled cola drinks in the world. The Pepsi-Cola trademark was registered in the U.S. Patent Office in 1903 (35 years ago).

**12 OUNCES**

**5¢**

## Pepsi-Cola

TRADE MARK REG. U.S. PAT. OFF. SINCE 1903

### TO DEALERS WHO SELL BEVERAGES

*Your greatest asset is the good-will of your customers.*

Pepsi-Cola is bottled under the most exacting sanitary conditions in OKLAHOMA CITY Every bottle is sterilized, and the contents are of uniform quality—pure, delicious and wholesome.

Pepsi-Cola offers no free goods, special discounts, nor premiums of any kind, but, instead, the very highest quality and value are packed into every 5¢ bottle — *Equal In All Respects To Any 10¢ Bottled Beverage On The Market.*

Pepsi-Cola *will pay* **FIVE THOUSAND DOLLARS ($5000.00)** *for proof to the contrary to any charity in* Oklahoma City.

HALL BEVERAGE CO.
Phone: 2-6078

**5¢**

When word spread of Pepsi-Cola's success, individuals lined up by the dozens to sign on as Pepsi-Cola distributors. During the Depression, jobs were scarce, and a Pepsi-Cola distributor could bring home a relatively good paycheck. Purchasing Pepsi-Cola directly from the bottling plant for 50 cents per case, distributors could unload those same cases for 75 cents throughout territories that were exclusively theirs. This distribution method kept Pepsi-Cola's sales force small—and its payroll down.

When Guth informed LaPides of his plan to build bottling plants at key locations around the country and then sell Pepsi-Cola through distributors, LaPides begged to differ. He argued that franchised bottlers who had a stake in making Pepsi-Cola successful would best ensure the company's growth. He also reminded Guth of the marketing value of bottlers who belonged to the communities they serviced.

Acquiescing to LaPides' knowledge of the bottling business, Guth made plans to franchise Pepsi-Cola bottlers throughout the United States. Yet, reluctant to stay entirely away from the bottling issue, Guth couldn't resist establishing a few company-owned plants, starting with eight—including the Long Island City, New York, plant—a number that today has mushroomed to several hundred.

Selling a larger-size bottle than one's competition for the same price requires an enormous volume to make a decent profit. Although the key to increasing volume may be mass advertising, customers must be assured they will be able to get their hands on the advertised product.

To ensure the availability of Pepsi-Cola, a massive campaign to enlist bottlers was launched. Territory representatives traveled from town to town on the lookout for

V.O. Robertson and his brother George franchised the Midwest for Pepsi-Cola in the 1930s and 1940s. Before becoming a territorial representative, V.O. Robertson had worked for Guth at Loft Inc.

Used beer bottles became the primary containers for Pepsi-Cola throughout the 1930s. The low cost made them a necessity for many bottlers.

*Today, a Pepsi-Cola franchise is worth millions of dollars, but in 1934, the price was $315. That was the cost of one unit of Pepsi-Cola concentrate.*

*The 12-ounce bottle quickly became the symbol of Pepsi-Cola's reemergence into the soft drink industry. This new bottle was painted on buildings, trucks, and company cars.*

worthy candidates. They were commissioned not only to sign up bottlers but also to guide recruits in growing their businesses. For their efforts, territory representatives were well rewarded, earning a royalty of two cents for every case sold in their territory—a relatively princely sum.

The roll call of territory representatives included Joe LaPides, who handled the mid-Atlantic states and the Southeast; George and V.O. Robertson, the Midwest and New England; and Clinton L. Jones, the West. The area immediately around New York was covered by the offices in Long Island City and a cadre of distributors.

Not surprisingly, Joe LaPides was the first to issue a franchise. On November 6, 1934, he appointed Pinnell Martin of Newville, Pennsylvania, a Pepsi-Cola bottler. At this time, the cost of obtaining a franchise was the purchase price of one unit of concentrate—$315—which would yield 1,200 cases of Pepsi-Cola. Also included in the purchase price were enough bottle caps and labels to produce 28,800 bottles.

The truth is, the profit on the sale of 12-ounce Pepsi-Cola bottles was so minuscule at first that many bottlers earned more on the deposit collected for the bottles. The used bottles, which cost $1 per gross,

produced $2.88 in revenues when deposits were collected. Admittedly, this may not seem like much money, but for many bottlers it made the difference in keeping their businesses in the black.

On May 29, 1934, a wholly owned subsidiary, Pepsi-Cola Company of Canada, Limited, was formed. By the end of 1934, Pepsi-Cola had turned the corner and was well on its way to becoming a phenomenal success. Business was so good that Guth was persuaded to open the first Pepsi-Cola plant outside the United States, in Montreal, Canada.

Yet, while Pepsi-Cola's fortunes were on the rise, Loft's were headed in the opposite direction. Guth may still have been president of Loft Inc., but he remained fixated on building and promoting Pepsi-Cola. By 1934, Loft's profits had sunk to $21,000. Finally, in 1935, Guth resigned as president and also from his seat on Loft's board of directors.

At a board meeting the following day, October 22, 1935, James W. Carkner

was elected president of Loft Inc. Guth, still a player with a third of Loft's outstanding stock, proposed that if Carkner would buy Guth's 200,000 shares of Loft Inc. for $3 each, he would refrain from challenging Carkner's presidency. Otherwise, Guth would move to replace him at the next stockholder meeting. Guth gave Carkner until December 31 to come up with the necessary $600,000.

This was not the only difficult position Guth had put Carkner in. Due to Guth's neglect, inventories at the Loft stores had fallen precariously low, especially with the Christmas season rapidly approaching. If those inventories weren't rebuilt in time to ensure healthy holiday sales, the company faced financial ruin.

Furthermore, an examination of the company's financial records revealed that $30,000 was missing from one of Loft's subsidiaries. It turned out that Guth had borrowed the money without paying it back. Anxious to avoid alienating those at Loft still loyal to Guth, Carkner sought outside legal counsel.

Carkner was referred to an attorney by the name of Herbert M. Singer of the firm Levien, Singer and Neuburger. Acknowledging the necessity for discretion, Singer agreed to review Loft's records in the evening, alone and in secret.

It didn't take long for Singer to conclude that Guth had used Loft's assets to obtain and grow his Pepsi-Cola business. Singer's advice to Carkner: pursue the issue in court. On Carkner's mind was Guth's threat of regaining control of Loft, which, among other things, would put an end to the lawsuit. Anxious that time was running out, Carkner green-lighted the move against Guth. On December 30, 1935, Loft Inc. filed suit against Charles Guth, Grace Company, and Pepsi-Cola, alleging that because Loft's assets had been used to acquire, build, and operate Pepsi-Cola, Pepsi-Cola legally belonged to Loft.

Guth figured his only recourse was to wrest control of Loft from Carkner, fire him and somehow get the lawsuit against him dropped. He presently controlled over 200,000 shares in Loft Inc., leaving 650,000 shares uncommitted. A proxy fight between Guth and Carkner loomed.

Neither Loft nor Carkner could afford a legal battle, let alone a proxy fight. Carkner had to agree to a contingency fee that, if the suit was successful, would grant his attorneys 25 percent of anything recovered—an agreement that would eventually land Singer on the board of directors of the Pepsi-Cola Company.

If Carkner expected to win a proxy fight, he would need some financial help. Because of the depressed value of Loft stock, a loan from a traditional financial institution was out of the question. He was instead directed to a firm by the name of Phoenix Securities.

Phoenix Securities, the brainchild of Wallace Groves and Walter S. Mack Jr., specialized in buying companies in financial trouble. After diagnosing a company's ills, they would apply a cure, and then sell the resuscitated enterprise—at a huge profit.

Such a scheme was exactly what Mack had in mind when he met with Carkner. Mack had no opinion whatsoever regarding Loft's lawsuit against Guth, nor did he

COPYRIGHT 1938 PEPSI-COLA CO.

Plant of the *Pepsi-Cola* Company of Canada, Ltd.

*Today, Pepsi-Cola is sold the world over and is universally recognized. This worldwide expansion began in 1934 with Pepsi-Cola's first bottling plant in Canada.*

*While James Carkner was busy trying to save Loft, Guth was expanding Pepsi-Cola all over the United States. Everywhere, people were drinking Pepsi-Cola from the new 12-ounce bottle.*

give Pepsi-Cola a second thought. However, he did see a chance of turning Loft around by persuading the confectioners to specialize in five-cent candy bars. Phoenix just happened to own a chain of stores called United Cigar-Whelan Stores that sold such bars—admittedly the candy business' most profitable item at the time. So, Phoenix Securities agreed to loan Loft Inc. $400,000 to be converted to Loft stock at Phoenix's request.

Phoenix was exactly what Carkner needed: an investor with pockets deep enough to win a proxy fight. In fact, Phoenix eventually bought up 31,000 shares of Loft stock to shore up support against Guth. When the board met in March 1936, Carkner and his supporters had the votes to maintain control of Loft.

Mack and Groves were consequently elected to Loft's board of directors. Meanwhile, the suit against Guth ground forward. Although some bottlers felt loyal to Guth due to business and family relationships, most bottlers remained neutral throughout the legal battle. Their primary concern was that it be resolved quickly so that the parent company could give their full attention to expansion.

The tricky part for Singer and his team was to convince the judge that although Loft Inc. never legally owned Pepsi-Cola, they did in fact own it, as they'd paid the company's start-up expenses under Guth. Somehow, Singer and his colleagues succeeded. The case ended on September 17, 1938, with the judge ruling for the plaintiff based on the conclusion that Pepsi-Cola's success depended on resources supplied by Loft.

The ruling was immediately appealed. The court appointed an interim board of directors to run Pepsi-Cola, consisting of three representatives from each side, with Walter Mack as president and Charles Guth as general manager. Despite a seventh director named by the court as an equalizing force, several months of heated board meetings ensued.

Finally, the Delaware Supreme Court announced its decision—it upheld the ruling for Loft. From this advantageous position, Loft engineered a court-approved settlement with Guth to stave off further appeals. Guth received an advisory contract for five years at $100,000 per year and a cash settlement. In addition, members of his family were awarded Pepsi-Cola franchises, his sons securing the Los Angeles area.

Court battles failed to arrest Pepsi-Cola's growth. New bottlers were continuously signing up, whether at national conventions or as a result of the tireless efforts of territory representatives. Models of ingenuity and perseverance, franchise appointees from 1935 to 1937 formed the backbone of the Pepsi-Cola bottler system over the next several decades. The number of Pepsi-Cola franchises in that same two-year period rose to 315, many remaining in families through subsequent generations.

Advertising in the latter half of the decade remained primitive. While some commercials were heard on radio, the bulk of Pepsi-Cola's advertising program was represented by newspaper ads. The Pepsi-Cola bottle was featured with the size and price highlighted. Displays and signs in retail outlets also contributed to making Pepsi-Cola a recognizable name.

Demand for Pepsi-Cola was soon straining the production capability of the 33rd Street plant. Fortunately, not too far away, the Socony Vacuum building was up for sale. This huge facility stood on a parcel of land adjacent to New York's East River.

In 1938, that facility became the new home of the Pepsi-Cola Company. Its great size enabled Guth to control various aspects of the business by bringing them under one roof. Buying and organizing the new plant was one of Guth's last acts at Pepsi-Cola.

*The battle for the control of Loft was really over who would own Pepsi-Cola. Guth therefore made an all-out effort to win the support of Loft stockholders.*

*As the battle raged between Loft and Guth, Pepsi-Cola continued to prosper. Sales steadily increased with the help of advertising promotional items such as this serving tray.*

By 1936, Pepsi-Cola was experiencing tremendous success with their five-cent 12-ounce bottle. Not surprisingly, a number of imitators tried to capitalize on the idea. Seizing the offensive, Pepsi-Cola emphasized that theirs was the original drink.

As this store window display demonstrates, the importance of the 12-ounce bottle to Pepsi-Cola's success in the mid- to late 1930s cannot be overstated.

*To satisfy the tremendous demand for Pepsi-Cola, Guth needed a new plant. In 1938, he converted this building into the world's largest bottling plant.*

The court ruling, which had already diminished his authority, soon resulted in his complete break with the company.

Eager for independence from the vagaries of the sugar industry, Guth installed a sugar refinery in the new plant, whose river access made it easy to bring in large shipments of sugar cane. To further assert his freedom from outside suppliers, Guth established a printing department to create Pepsi-Cola bottle labels and other advertising materials in-house. Caps and bottle cases were also produced in the new plant. Primarily, the plant housed a substantial bottling operation, employing, among others, bottle washers and bottle labelers. In fact, Pepsi-Cola's new Long Island City facility was billed as the world's largest soft drink plant.

Although some may brand Charles Guth the villain of this period of Pepsi-Cola history, a good case can be made otherwise. The argument for numbering Guth among the heroes stems from his determination and deep desire to make Pepsi-Cola a success. Guth's single-mindedness may have been at the heart of his troubles, but it was this focus that helped boost the fortunes of Pepsi-Cola. During the height of the Depression, Guth had managed to sell a cola drink made by a company that had twice gone bankrupt.

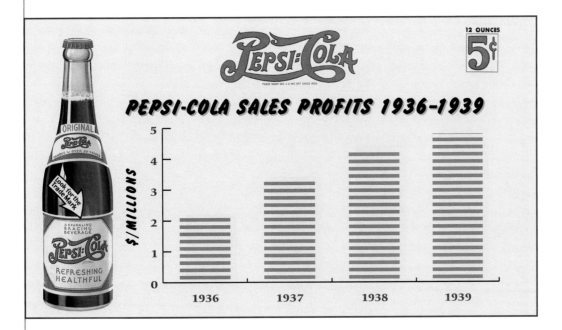

Whatever blunders had resulted from his blind ambition, he paid the ultimate price when he lost control of Pepsi-Cola—the company he'd almost single-handedly resurrected.

In any event, it cannot be denied that with Guth at the helm, for the first time since the early days of Pepsi-Cola, the company was turning a substantial profit.

*Forced to give up his claim to ownership of Pepsi-Cola, Charles Guth tried to start another soft drink company. It was called Mavis Cola, Mavis being the name he had used for his candy business.*

Unloading Raw Sugar at **Pepsi-Cola** Sugar Refinery

*Sugar remained one of the most important ingredients in the manufacture of Pepsi-Cola. To ensure a ready supply of sugar, Pepsi-Cola built their own refinery at the Long Island City bottling plant.*

Jerry Cooke

# bigger drink, better taste

Pepsi-Cola headed into a new decade with brand-new management. Phoenix Securities, which owned 29 percent of Loft Inc. and a controlling interest in the company, took it upon themselves to name the president of Pepsi-Cola. In their estimation, Phoenix Securities vice president Walter S. Mack Jr. was the individual best equipped to lead Pepsi-Cola into the future. Thus, in July 1939, Mack assumed the position of president and chief executive officer of the Pepsi-Cola Company.

At first, Mack made a heroic attempt to divide his time between Pepsi-Cola and Phoenix Securities. Eventually, though, he resigned from Phoenix Securities, resulting in the dissolution of the firm and Mack obtaining shares in the Pepsi-Cola Company through the Loft connection.

Mack was now free to devote himself full time to Pepsi-Cola, which needed serious attending to. Sales had indeed skyrocketed with the introduction of the nickel 12-ounce bottle. But, as Mack realized, sustained growth demanded aggressive nationwide marketing. This necessitated improving Pepsi-Cola's public image, which for years had been tarnished by the appropriation of used beer bottles as well as by inconsistent advertising. Additionally, Pepsi-Cola bottlers were in need of an efficiency boost, courtesy of the latest management techniques.

First, Mack tackled the management situation. Guth had pretty much run a one-person shop, making all major decisions himself and decreeing that employees report directly to him. Mack delegated responsibility to a team of old and new managers, leaving himself to oversee advertising.

In the past, advertising had been handled in-house, from copy to artwork. An agency was used sparingly to secure print ad space and radio time and to

*Through the late 1930s and early 1940s, Pepsi-Cola's most prominent features were a 12-ounce bottle and a five-cent price.*

*Opposite: Walter Mack, a venture capitalist, entered the Pepsi-Cola story purely by accident, serving as president of the company from 1939 to 1950.*

*Skywriting debuted as an advertising tool by Pepsi-Cola in 1939. The name Pepsi-Cola, spelled out in the sky, attracted the attention of onlookers—as well as newspaper reporters.*

transforming each one into an ardent salesperson. Representatives also guided bottlers in the optimal use of advertising as well as in ways to create venues in which the public could sample Pepsi-Cola.

All of this effort paid off. Bottlers gained confidence that Pepsi-Cola was a product that could compete against Coca-Cola, which had dominated the cola market for years. Statistics bore this out: in 1939, sales of Pepsi-Cola shot up 39 percent. This success was achieved with an advertising budget of $600,000, compared to an estimated $15 million spent by Coca-Cola.

Pepsi-Cola's success led to a flurry of imitators. Not only was the pressure on Pepsi-Cola to loosen Coca-Cola's stranglehold on soft drink sales but also to distinguish its product from an increasing number of colas crowding the market. Mack was well aware of the need for Pepsi-Cola to advertise in a big and bold way.

One of the advertising schemes that Mack inherited from Charles Guth was skywriting. Skywriting had been developed during World War I as a way of communicating with ground troops but was never widely used. Its commercial application was patented and therefore not fully exploited.

Writing in the sky was at the time such a rare occurrence that it generated free publicity for Pepsi-Cola. It was also pretty spectacular. Each letter measured up to a mile in height, while the name Pepsi-Cola stretched for six miles. Indeed, one woman in New York even phoned the company, informing them that God had just written their product's name over the city.

Mack was so pleased with the results of the skywriting program that he expanded it, and through most of the 1940s the Pepsi

perform routine work. Mack enlisted several prominent advertising firms to propose advertising campaigns. The Newell-Emmet agency ended up winning the Pepsi-Cola account based on Mack's feel for the working relationship he could expect from them. Mack understood that to grab public attention and secure name recognition, Pepsi-Cola would need to blaze new trails in advertising.

Mack also understood that Pepsi-Cola's success depended on the commitment of bottlers. To company representatives went the task of generating enthusiasm about the product among bottlers, with the goal of

Skywriter flew as a promotional tool. In the 1970s, the company revived the practice, and it remains in use by Pepsi bottlers today to draw attention to anniversaries and other celebrations.

As attention-getting as skywriting was, one of Pepsi-Cola's most successful advertising campaigns remains the endearing Pepsi and Pete, the Pepsi-Cola cops. These hugely popular cartoon characters premiered in 1939.

Mack's aim had been to create advertising that would appeal to entire families. He first planned to buy the rights to Popeye the spinach-eating sailor, but initial talks about licensing the comic strip star indicated that this would break Pepsi-Cola's budget.

The ad agency offered myriad alternatives in cartoon representatives—everything from bears to angelic children. Nothing seemed right until someone proposed characters similar to the Keystone Kops in the silent comedy films of Mack Sennett. Walter Mack liked the idea of policemen protecting the good name and quality of Pepsi-Cola. In fact, early Pepsi and Pete ads declared that each bottle of Pepsi-Cola tasted good and contained 12 full ounces.

Mack himself named the two characters Pepsi and Pete. They became such a hit with the public that after just two years, they were numbered among the most recognized advertising characters in America. Featured in the Sunday newspaper cartoon pages, Pepsi and Pete also appeared in magazine ads and on display material wherever Pepsi-Cola was sold. Their popularity grew to the point that actors were hired to make personal appearances as the lovable duo.

Pepsi and Pete arrived on the scene about the same time as Pepsi-Cola's most effective advertising tool—the Pepsi-Cola

jingle. From 1937 to 1938, Pepsi-Cola advertised its product through standard radio commercials, whereby copy written by an ad agency was read in a voice calculated to grab the attention of listeners. Mack wanted Pepsi-Cola commercials to be more lively and memorable, so he requested that the agency come up with a jingle. Two songwriters, Alan B. Kent and Austin H. Croom-Johnson, presented Mack with an appropriately catchy ditty.

Mack took his innovation one step farther by stripping down the commercial to a 15-second spot, consisting only of the jingle. Adhering to the principle that the

*In 1939, Pepsi-Cola diverged from the standard radio advertising format to introduce a short jingle. The Pepsi-Cola jingle would become the most successful radio ad of all time. Listeners went so far as to praise its entertainment value.*

*Pepsi-Cola's success in the 1940s depended, in part, on bottlers investing in bottles and crates to improve Pepsi's image.*

words. Mack had gotten just what he wanted—Pepsi-Cola had become a household name.

While advertising did wonders for Pepsi's name recognition, improving the product's image would require more drastic measures. Since the introduction of the 12-ounce Pepsi-Cola for five cents, the company had purchased only used bottles, fulfilling management's two most important requirements at the time: the bottles must hold 12 ounces, and they must be cheap. When used beer bottles were lacking, some bottlers resorted to whatever was available, including used ketchup bottles.

Besides having a somewhat checkered history, the used bottles came in a bewildering array of colors, with brown being the most common for beer bottles, though they could also be green or even clear. Mack understood that presenting the consumer with varying bottle colors as well as shapes worked against the goal of building a loyal customer base—Pepsi's inconsistent appearance eroded product recognition.

Mack's solution was to hire Louis Carr, the designer responsible for the interior of Tiffany's in New York, to create a new Pepsi-Cola bottle. This was exactly what Pepsi-Cola needed—a recognizable symbol for an emerging cola company. Carr's bottle design sported a Pepsi-Cola label on the neck and body, with the product name blown onto the shoulder glass. This new bottle made its debut in early 1940, with a strong push from the Pepsi-Cola Company for every bottler to adopt its use.

The introduction of Pepsi-Cola's new bottle design ushered in what may have been Pepsi-Cola's golden era of in-store advertising, funded by the tidy profits the company enjoyed from 1938 and 1939. Enormous metal signs and fine lithographs

customer is always right, the advertising people, appalled at Mack's radical approach, nonetheless acquiesced.

Mack's instincts were vindicated when the public embraced the ad. People everywhere seemed to be singing or at least humming the Pepsi-Cola jingle. It even became a jukebox selection. In fact, the jingle was played so often over its 10 years on the air that even today, more than 50 years later, people who heard it still remember the depicting exquisite females were produced by such celebrated artists as George Petty. Pepsi-Cola's name appeared on every type of store display and novelty item used to promote soft drinks.

Mack decided the time had come to complete the franchising of the entire country, begun in 1934. The Pepsi-Cola Company and its representatives made a concerted effort to ensure Pepsi-Cola's availability in every state, and indeed, they were close to establishing bottlers from coast to coast.

Pepsi-Cola was on a roll. A skillfully employed barrage of advertising was having tremendous results. Sales—and profits— were on the increase. Pepsi-Cola was on its way toward becoming a leading soft drink company, and Mack was convinced it was only a matter of time before they would give Coca-Cola a run for their money.

Yet, while marketing and sales flourished, the company was beleaguered once again by a lawsuit with the cola giant. In 1938, Coca-Cola filed suit against Pepsi-Cola for trademark infringement. No doubt such legal action came as a result of Pepsi-Cola's success. Coca-Cola, feeling threatened by the increase in Pepsi-Cola sales, attempted to stop their competitor in court.

Coca-Cola argued that because cola was part of their registered trademark, any use of that word infringed on Coca-Cola's name. Coca-Cola solicited the court to prohibit the Pepsi-Cola Company from using the Pepsi-Cola name.

*Volume was key to Pepsi-Cola's ability to make a profit, and nothing was better suited to creating volume than the six-bottle carton.*

# pepsi and pete, the pepsi-cola cops

Pepsi and Pete, the Pepsi-Cola cops, were featured by Pepsi-Cola from 1939 through 1951. Over the years, they were rendered by a number of illustrators, including the famed Rube Goldberg. The popular duo appeared in newspapers and magazines, and Pepsi and Pete animated commercials were shown in movie theaters during the 1940s.

Legally speaking, the case looked grim for Pepsi-Cola. The Coca-Cola Company appeared to have precedent on its side, providing mountains of evidence that the courts had consistently upheld their right to cola as part of their trademark. Pepsi-Cola would somehow have to refute a formidable file of previous court decisions.

Just when the case appeared to be lost, Mack received a phone call from a woman in New Jersey by the name of Mrs. Herman Smith. Mrs. Smith's late husband had been the founder and owner of a small soft drink company called Cleo-Cola. Smith expressed to Mack how sorry she was that Coca-Cola was set on putting Pepsi-Cola out of business—the way they had Cleo-Cola. Mack replied that he believed cola was a generic term referring to the kola nut. Mrs. Smith responded that while her husband had been of the same opinion, Coca-Cola had nonetheless railroaded him out of business—and, by the way, she still had the photograph of the $35,000 check they gave him.

Mack was astounded at what he had heard. Nothing in the court record mentioned Coca-Cola presenting Cleo-Cola with a check for $35,000. Moreover, examination of the photograph furnished by Mrs. Smith revealed that the account number written on the check was H13. Believing this to be the code for Coca-Cola's legal department, the Pepsi-Cola attorney figured that the Coca-Cola Company had probably settled many such trademark infringement lawsuits out of court in a similar manner. Settling out of court was not the same as winning a verdict that declared that cola was part and parcel of the Coca-Cola trademark.

Pepsi-Cola's attorney immediately petitioned the court to obtain the ledgers for the H-13 account. Coca-Cola's lawyers thereupon requested a three-day adjournment. Mack's autobiography describes what happened next. According to Mack, Robert Woodruff, the president of Coca-Cola, approached him and proposed that, legal squabbling being bad for business, they end it then and there. Mack agreed—if Coca-Cola would formally

recognize Pepsi-Cola's trademark. Woodruff was amenable, and letters were signed acknowledging the right of each company to use their respective trademarks. Meanwhile, the theory persists that the Coca-Cola Company ended their lawsuit against Pepsi-Cola to keep their legal department ledgers shrouded in secrecy.

In any case, the Coca-Cola Company of Canada, determining that the agreement between Woodruff and Mack applied only to the United States, challenged the Pepsi-Cola trademark in that nation, suing Pepsi-Cola of Canada Ltd. for infringement. Coca-Cola won the first round, sending Pepsi-Cola to appeal to the Canadian Supreme Court. The Canadian Supreme Court reversed the lower court decision, agreeing with Pepsi-Cola that *cola* refers generically to the kola nut, an ingredient used in all cola drinks.

Coca-Cola, unwilling to accept defeat, appealed to the Privy Council in London, the highest court of the British Commonwealth (of which Canada was a member). The onset of World War II complicated Pepsi-Cola's efforts to secure legal representation overseas. Mack, determined to be well represented in London, retained Wendell

Willkie as Pepsi-Cola's attorney for the case. A former presidential candidate and political rival who nevertheless had become friendly with President Franklin Roosevelt, Willkie persuaded Roosevelt to send him to London on a military transport, ostensibly to promote the sale of war bonds. While in London, Willkie appealed before the Privy Council on behalf of Pepsi-Cola. Once again, Pepsi-Cola prevailed. No longer would the company's trademark be in dispute.

Despite potential legal entanglements, Pepsi-Cola continued to expand beyond the borders of the United States. Bradham had set the ball rolling by registering the Pepsi-Cola trademark in other countries. Guth then initiated plans to operate bottling plants abroad. By 1939, Pepsi-Cola had facilities in Great Britain and Cuba. In Canada, business had grown so that by the end of 1938, 85 Pepsi-Cola bottlers were operating throughout the provinces.

By 1940, the Pepsi-Cola trademark was registered in more than 80 countries, including the Soviet Union in 1938. It would not be until decades later, however, that bottling took place on Russian soil.

The only real difficulty facing Pepsi-Cola was Loft Inc., its parent company. Pepsi-Cola's profits were subsidizing huge losses by Loft. Plans were made to merge Loft into Pepsi-Cola Company until a review by the Internal Revenue Service revealed that such a merger would constitute a taxable reorganization. Tax laws being what they are, if the merger went the other way, taxation would not apply. Not surprisingly, Pepsi-Cola merged into Loft Inc.

This merger, duly approved by Loft stockholders on May 29, 1941, resulted in the Pepsi-Cola Company becoming Loft Inc. Loft Inc. then changed its name to Pepsi-Cola. With this name change the Pepsi-Cola Company was listed on the New York Stock Exchange for the first time.

Pepsi-Cola had become a formidable competitor in the cold bottle market, whereby a customer buys a cold soft drink for immediate consumption. In 1938, Pepsi-Cola sold more than 180 million bottles in the New York area alone and comparable results were being achieved by many Pepsi-Cola bottlers throughout the country. The next challenge: to go after the newly emerging take-home market.

In the beginning, soft drinks were sold a drink at a time, either by the glass or by the bottle. With the increasing presence of refrigerators in homes came a new market for beverages that could be taken home and stored for later consumption. To supply this market, Pepsi-Cola introduced the six-bottle carton in late 1939, accompanied by a flurry of advertising programs and in-store displays.

The take-home market lent itself to Pepsi-Cola's image as an affordable product. Homemakers looking for ways to stretch their household budget could save by purchasing the soft drink by the carton, which sold for 25 cents, or less than a nickel a bottle.

In 1940, Pepsi-Cola produced an electrical cooler that could double as a vending machine. While Coca-Cola had already placed 8,000 of these marvels of convenience by 1937, this marked the beginning of Pepsi-Cola's use of vending machines, which would become a significant sales tool for the company.

In 1940, profits for Pepsi-Cola reached $8.5 million. Just a year later, they soared to $14.9 million. Advertising undoubtedly contributed to the increase in sales. Route

*Collecting used bottle caps became part of the Pepsi-Cola delivery person's everyday routine during World War II.*

*To promote the new six-bottle carton, some bottlers employed specially built delivery trucks. Praised for its stamina as well as its carrying capacity, this vehicle won the endorsement of the president of the Montgomery, Alabama, Pepsi-Cola Bottling Company for averaging 44$^1/_2$ miles per gallon on a 450-mile trip.*

ICE COLD

HITS THE SPOT

*Super Icer*

*Electric coolers and vending machines contributed to the expansion of Pepsi-Cola into new markets and locations.*

*Pepsi-Cola developed a strategy of targeting advertising to a magazine's core audience. For Life, they supplied family-oriented ads, while for Esquire, they addressed more adult themes.*

salespeople could avail themselves of training programs offered by the parent company to spruce up their presentation skills when calling on customers. Bottlers, for their part, had been quick to convert over to the new Pepsi-Cola bottle and to modernize their plants to meet consumer demand. Pepsi-Cola's future looked bright indeed.

Then, on December 7, 1941, the Japanese bombed Pearl Harbor, precipitating the entry of the United States into World War II. Just as World War I had caused severe shortages in manpower, materials, and sugar, so did World War II. As a result, Pepsi-Cola's profits for the decade were greatest in 1941. Each year from 1942 to 1946, profits dropped markedly. The margins improved slightly by 1947, but it would take until 1955 for profits to equal those of 1941.

During the war, the nation's security was at risk, and every citizen and business was duty bound to contribute to its defense. Pepsi-Cola began producing ads that, in addition to proclaiming the goodness of Pepsi, encouraged citizens to buy liberty bonds to aid the war effort. To emphasize a patriotic spirit, the company adopted red, white, and blue as its corporate colors.

Pepsi-Cola honored its franchise agreements—even while the franchise operators went off to war. One such franchise agreement involved Fred Nackard of Flagstaff, Arizona. At the start of World War II, Nackard was bottling a competitive brand. When he entered the Army, he wrote a letter to the parent company asking their assurance that they would not cancel his franchise while he fought for his country. A company representative responded that he couldn't promise anything of the sort.

*"But you didn't have to deliver it yourself, Mr. Schmidlip!"*

Recalling Pepsi's attempts to recruit him a few years earlier, Nackard promptly contacted the company. Pepsi-Cola put together a franchise agreement that Nackard signed while in basic training at Ft. Lewis, Washington—an agreement that remains in effect today, as the Pepsi-Cola franchise in Flagstaff continues to be owned and operated by the Nackard family.

Walter Mack's greatest challenge during the war years was keeping the Pepsi-Cola Company operating. Finding enough raw materials to supply Pepsi bottlers was his number one job during the war. A lack of such materials would stymie production of Pepsi, causing orders for Pepsi-Cola concentrate to plummet. If Pepsi-Cola couldn't sell concentrate, the company would go out of business. Bottlers needed bottles, sugar, truck tires, and parts for their equipment.

Most Pepsi-Cola bottling plants were family businesses, which, in many cases, had been started up using a family's life savings. Keeping those businesses functioning during the war years became a family effort. Grandparents, wives, and children went to work at Pepsi-Cola plants to keep them operating. When the Irvin brothers, who owned the Pepsi-Cola bottling plant in Bloomington, Illinois, joined the army, their father quit his own job to keep the franchise going.

After the war, when Maurice Irvin called on a mom-and-pop store whose supply of Pepsi had been interrupted during his enlistment, he was asked to explain the disruption in service. To Irvin's response that he had been proudly serving in the army, the store owner retorted, "That is no excuse—we need Pepsi-Cola!"

During World War II, when metal was needed for everything from rifles to battleships, its civilian use was limited to businesses deemed essential to the war effort. While many Pepsi-Cola drinkers might argue otherwise, supplying the soft drink business was a low priority. As a result, the bottle cap, one of the most important components of the bottling business, was in short supply.

Pepsi-Cola began recycling used bottle caps, setting up collection bins wherever Pepsi was sold. Route salesmen would collect the caps and return them to the plant where, in many cases, the caps would be refurbished by the bottler's children.

*During World War II, Pepsi-Cola produced ads geared to bolstering the confidence and morale of the American public.*

*Many of the company's ads during the 1940s were designed to make Pepsi-Cola a nationally recognized name.*

Fred Nackard signed his Pepsi-Cola franchise agreement while in the Army. His wife, Monica, operated the plant while he served his country.

Bottlers like the Irvin Brothers of Bloomington, Illinois, went off to war while their families kept their Pepsi-Cola franchise operating.

TEMPTY ...TASTY

PEPSI-COLA COMPANY

Annual Report
1943

Gasoline was another product that was rationed during the war. Procuring enough gas to run delivery trucks posed a serious problem for the Pepsi-Cola Company and its bottlers. The Long Island City Pepsi-Cola plant came up with the clever solution of employing barges to drop off Pepsi-Cola at key locations along the East River.

Of all the wartime shortages, the rationing of sugar was by far the most trying for the company. Sugar allotments were based on usage in previous years, so rationing regulations worked against most Pepsi-Cola bottlers. Being newly recruited, the majority hadn't built up enough business to ensure that their quota of sugar would meet current demand. The problem was critical, as the responsibility for adding sugar to the concentrate supplied

... BETWEEN TAKES THEY TAKE TO Pepsi-Cola

The "movie lots" in Hollywood are going Pepsi-Cola in a great big way. Different from other cola drinks, Pepsi-Cola appeals because of its *finer flavor*. Each big bottle pours 12 full ounces . . . a generous helping that really quenches thirst. Enjoy America's BIG favorite—*go* Pepsi-Cola now.

Pepsi-Cola is made only by Pepsi-Cola Company, Long Island City, N. Y. and is bottled locally by authorized bottlers from coast to coast.

Edmond O'Brien and Lucille Ball starred in RKO-Radio Pictures' current hit "A Girl, A Guy and A Gob"

A SPARKLING BEVERAGE

5¢
12 OZ. BOTTLE

*FREE: Pepsi-Cola recipe booklet . . . write Pepsi-Cola Company, Long Island City, N. Y. Dept. H.*

94

by the Pepsi-Cola Company fell solely upon the bottler's shoulders. Some bottlers even ignored the prescribed formula for blending Pepsi-Cola syrup, making quality control impossible.

Mack understood that while requiring bottlers to acquire and pay for their own sugar supply benefited the parent company, the Pepsi-Cola Company would in fact suffer if bottlers lacked the sugar necessary to produce their product to company standards. So the Pepsi-Cola Company began to assist bottlers in obtaining this crucial ingredient.

Almost immediately after the start of the war, Mack purchased 86,000 tons of sugar to be stored at the Long Island City plant, with the aim of protecting Pepsi-Cola bottlers from sugar shortages. The government, however, promptly stepped in and demanded 40,000 tons of the sugar for defense purposes.

Mack then proceeded to purchase a sugar plantation in Cuba for the exclusive use

*Women as well as boys not old enough for military duty kept many Pepsi-Cola plants operating throughout World War II.*

*As in World War I, disruption of the sugar supply became a major dilemma for Pepsi-Cola during World War II.*

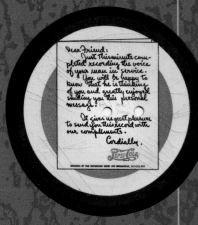

Every Pepsi-Cola center

for servicemen housed a

recording studio where

military personnel could

record their voice on a

78 record to send to

loved ones. Pepsi-Cola

called these voice letters.

TIMES SQUARE SERVICE MEN'S CENTER, BROADWAY AT 47th STREET, NEW YORK CITY

PEPSI-COLA CENTER FOR SERVICE MEN AND WOMEN, 13th AND G STS., N.W., WASHINGTON, D. C.

The Times Square Pepsi-Cola Center for Servicemen was one of three sponsored by Pepsi-

Cola. These centers offered a refuge for military personnel far from home.

The 1943 Congressional Record documents Pepsi-Cola's service to the country through

these centers.

of the Pepsi-Cola Company. But the U.S. government maintained that Cuban sugar also came under the jurisdiction of the rationing laws.

The indefatigable Mack devised yet another plan. Learning that an abundance of sugar could be had in Mexico, he determined to buy it and import it in syrup form. To Pepsi-Cola's knowledge, there was no law against the importation of flavored syrup. A syrup-processing facility was set up in Monterrey, Mexico, close enough to the U.S. border to provide ease of transportation.

For the most part, the Mexican Pepsi-Cola syrup, called El Masco, helped keep many bottlers operating, though some said it gave Pepsi-Cola a bad taste. The

MADE *RIGHT*
WHILE YOU WATCH

FOUNTAIN...

**Pepsi·Cola**

TRADE MARK REG.

BIG TEN-OUNCE GLASS

*Because the war made it impossible for Pepsi-Cola to obtain new fountain dispensing equipment, the product was mixed by hand.*

their own brand of carbonated drinks quit bottling those in order to devote their entire supply of sugar to bottling Pepsi-Cola. Some bartered and traded with other businesses to obtain the sugar necessary to keep operating. Such efforts paid off, and most Pepsi-Cola franchises survived World War II. Confidence was high that when the war was over, Pepsi-Cola would resume its fast-paced growth.

The setting up of Pepsi-Cola centers for servicemen was one of the most popular programs sponsored by the company to bolster the war effort. The first center opened in July 1942 in New York City's Times Square, followed by others in Washington, D.C., and San Francisco. All operating expenses were paid by the Pepsi-Cola Company.

In their first year of operation, the centers attracted more than two million visitors from every branch of the military. For the convenience of military personnel, doors stayed open from 9:30 A.M. until 12:30 A.M. During those hours, men and women in the armed forces were served hamburgers and sandwiches at reduced prices—and all the free Pepsi-Cola they could drink. Every center was equipped with showers and telephones. One letter— written on servicemen center stationery, addressed to "Fuzzy Kitten" and signed "Your loving fiancé"—describes the ballad "Night and Day" being played over the radio, adding, "It has all the words the way I feel about you, Darling."

Perhaps the most popular feature of the centers was the voice recording booth. Free of charge, visitors were invited to record a personal message onto a 78 record to send home to friends and family. For the tongue-tied, scripts were provided to help put their feelings into words.

use of El Masco came to an end in late 1944, when the U.S. government ruled that its use violated restriction laws on the importation of sugar. This decision was based on an interpretation of the law that determined that while Pepsi-Cola may not have violated the letter of the law, the company was not in compliance with its spirit.

The bottlers wisely did not wait for the parent company to provide them with all the sugar they might require. Many who had also been in the business of selling

With the success of its 12-ounce bottle, Pepsi-Cola had all but abandoned the fountain business. However, with the soft drink's growing popularity came more and more requests for Pepsi at fountain counters. To give the public what it wanted—and to open a new market for Pepsi-Cola—Mack and the board of directors decided to once again offer Pepsi-Cola as a fountain drink. A bonus would be the opportunity for Pepsi-Cola to gain new customers around the country.

The problem was that it was 1942, and the materials needed for manufacturing fountain dispensing equipment were scarce. After much deliberation, the Pepsi-Cola management came up with a solution. Pepsi-Cola syrup would be provided to fountain operators in 12-ounce bottles, which would be poured into Pepsi-Cola glasses specially marked to show how far to fill them with the syrup. The glasses were sold or given away to fountain operators. When carbonated water was mixed in, *voilá*, a glass of Pepsi was yours. Instructions were printed on the back of the syrup bottles.

With bottled syrup eliminating the need for special equipment, Pepsi-Cola moved ahead with plans to capture the fountain trade. The first test market was Binghamton, New York, and the response was positive. Next up for product testing was Miami, Florida, where the results were encouraging enough to convince Pepsi-Cola to supply its syrup to fountains across the nation. Nevertheless, Pepsi-Cola fountain sales remained modest during this time, due to the lack of modern dispensers used by the competition.

World War II ended in August 1945, leaving Pepsi-Cola eager to resume normal operations. Postwar plans included modernizing bottle plants, expanding the foun-

tain business, and developing the use of vending machines. But these plans did not account for postwar inflation, and plant modernization was postponed until a more favorable economic climate developed.

Also not taken into account was continued sugar rationing. To prevent profiteering, the government maintained sugar restrictions until 1947, effectively preventing Pepsi-Cola from regaining the growth rate it had enjoyed prior to the war. Production at most Pepsi-Cola bottling facilities hovered far below capacity due in part to sugar restrictions.

To increase production without an increased sugar supply, Pepsi-Cola in 1946 introduced a new product, sugar-free

*Pepsi-Cola introduced Evervess, a sparkling water, in 1946. This marked the company's first attempt at marketing a noncola drink.*

*Pepsi-Cola was made from concentrate that was shipped to bottlers in 10-gallon barrels.*

*World War II and postwar inflation took its toll on bottlers, but many of those who were able to hang in would eventually prosper.*

*By 1949, inflation led Pepsi-Cola to sell its 12-ounce bottle for six cents. Advertising downplayed price and emphasized quantity.*

Evervess sparkling water. Pepsi-Cola bottlers already had on hand everything they needed to bottle the beverage. Production of Evervess appeared to be an ingenious way to boost sales. However, marketed to a more affluent class of people, the luxury image of the product never caught on.

While sugar restrictions hampered sales of Pepsi-Cola during and just after the war, postwar inflation proved a more serious nemesis. Between 1941 and 1947, the cost of living in the United States increased by 52 percent, while Pepsi-Cola continued to sell its 12-ounce bottles for five cents a piece. Something had to be done, because it was only a matter of time before Pepsi's profits would be eaten away by inflation.

The central debate was whether to

Pepsi's Best... Take No Less

*To be competitive in the on-premises and vending machine markets, Pepsi-Cola offered a five-cent drink in an eight-ounce bottle.*

increase the price of Pepsi-Cola or decrease the bottle size. The regional and economic diversity of the communities served by Pepsi-Cola bottlers caused both solutions to be adopted. Bottlers who felt obligated to maintain the nickel price offered a 10-ounce bottle. Those who were confident that a price increase of a penny would meet only minor resistance continued to offer a 12-ounce bottle.

Most Pepsi-Cola customers believed that even at six cents, a 12-ounce Pepsi was

*The popular Pepsi-Cola jingle spilled over into a series of Pepsi-Cola magazine ads in 1947.*

*Pepsi-Cola was first offered in cans in 1949, without much success. Military installations excepted, Pepsi-Cola would not again be available in cans until 1960.*

*Pepsi-Cola's competitiveness in the vending machine market was hampered by the cost and size of the bottle, so they developed a cup vending machine. But it never caught on with consumers.*

still a bargain. Nevertheless, the competition proceeded to attack Pepsi-Cola for raising its price. Dealers were advised not to accept the penny increase in order to force the company to roll back the price. According to at least one Pepsi-Cola bottler, the local bottler for Coca-Cola tried to persuade retailers not to buy Pepsi-Cola because selling a soft drink for more than five cents was unpatriotic.

Pepsi-Cola's greatest marketing strategy, pricing, was now working against the company. The nickel era of Pepsi-Cola had come to an end.

It did not die easily. Cutting into a profit margin already decimated by post-war inflation, Pepsi-Cola increased the price of its concentrate, which forced bottlers to devote more of their business to flavored drinks in order to recoup their losses. This in turn hurt the sales of Pepsi concentrate.

In an effort to reverse the slump in sales, New York lowered the price they charged bottlers for the Pepsi-Cola concentrate. This was done at a time when profits were already precariously low because of

plunging sales. Raising and then lowering the price of Pepsi-Cola concentrate dealt a severe blow to the finances of the Pepsi-Cola Company. By 1949, the future of the company was in doubt.

Pepsi-Cola began to refocus its advertising away from pricing toward taste and size. New ads trumpeted Pepsi's value in terms of its larger size—even at 10 ounces, it was still bigger than its chief competitor. Slogans like PEPSI'S BEST, WHY TAKE LESS? and MORE BOUNCE TO THE OUNCE reinforced the size comparison without mentioning price.

Also during this inflationary period, Pepsi-Cola began expanding its vending machine market. This was difficult to do with the 12-ounce bottle due to its maximum size and minimal profit margin. Vending machines were designed to take nickels, so raising the price to six or seven cents would prove impractical.

Pepsi-Cola resolved the dilemma by introducing an eight-ounce bottle that could be sold profitably in a nickel vending machine. The eight-ounce bottle was called an "on-premises" bottle because it could be sold not only in vending machines but also at sporting events and in movie theaters—anywhere a captive audience was willing to pay five cents for eight ounces of a soft drink.

The other soft drink packaging innovation introduced during this period was the use of cans. Americans had become more attracted to convenience over savings in the products that they purchased. Responding to this trend, in 1949 Pepsi-Cola test-marketed a 12-ounce can priced at 10 cents. While available for a couple of years, such packaging never caught on. Public acceptance of soft drinks in cans was several decades down the road.

Pepsi-Cola had begun the decade with record profits and buoyant optimism, confident that the dream of becoming a great soft drink company would soon be a reality. By the late 1940s, however, Pepsi-Cola was again on the brink of financial ruin. The expected postwar economic boom would be delayed, and inflation sabotaged company profits.

Volume had always been Pepsi-Cola's key to success. As sales slumped, making a profit selling Pepsi seemed next to impossible. Reduced profits meant less advertising, which cut sales further. No plan was forthcoming to halt the plummeting sales.

Nevertheless, most bottlers remained committed to the product. Convinced that Pepsi-Cola was still the best cola drink in the world, most bottlers had invested their life savings in Pepsi-Cola. They had survived tough times before, and would have to do so again.

*The Pepsi-Cola promotion of 1947 was the Treasure Top contest. Cash prizes, awarded to individuals who collected specially marked bottle caps, ended up totaling more than $200,000.*

*Originally, Pepsi-Cola sold for 10 cents a can or three for a quarter. Today, these cone-top cans are sought after by collectors, normally selling for several hundred dollars each.*

# the light refreshment

A new decade again dawned with someone new at the helm of Pepsi-Cola. Although Walter Mack had navigated the company through some of its greatest successes as well as challenges, sales and profits continued to decline, forcing the Pepsi-Cola board of directors to make a change.

That change came on March 5, 1950, when the board appointed Mack chairman. But, missing the challenges he had relished as president, Mack relinquished the chairmanship after just a few months and was replaced by James Carkner. Mack would, however, serve as a paid consultant to the company until 1957.

Now captaining the company as president was Alfred N. Steele. Born in Nashville, Tennessee, Steele had graduated from Northwestern University in 1923. After various jobs, he landed a position with D'Arcy, the advertising firm that handled the Coca-Cola account. In 1945, he accepted a vice presidency with the Coca-Cola Company.

Considered by many to be an advertising genius, Steele was a master at staging events that garnered publicity for him as well as for his product. He never quite fit in at Coca-Cola—his brash flamboyant style was not taken kindly to within the company's staid walls. Eventually, Steele was estranged from the day-to-day operations of the company.

Pepsi-Cola was well aware of Steele's talents. Learning that he'd fallen out of favor with Coca-Cola management, Pepsi promptly offered him a job. In 1949, Steele accepted the invitation and became a vice president at Pepsi-Cola.

During this period, the mere mention of Pepsi warranted a pink slip at Coca-Cola. After Steele had left, mention of his name, too, resulted in Coca-Cola employees being shown the exit. In the wake of the court battles of the 1930s and 1940s, the rivalry between the two cola companies remained

*Soft drinks were traditionally a summer drink, but in the 1950s Pepsi began an advertising program designed to make the public buy Pepsi throughout the year.*

*Developing new markets in which to sell Pepsi-Cola was an ongoing effort. Pepsi was there when commercial advertising began to expand in the 1950s.*

fierce. Tensions escalated when Steele left Coca-Cola, taking many of the company's rising stars with him.

Whatever ire Pepsi-Cola incurred from its rival was worth it, considering that, like his predecessors, Steele was the right leader at the right time for the company. Steele's experience at Coca-Cola made him an expert on the operations of the soft drink industry. What Pepsi-Cola needed at the time was a company head who understood the inner workings of the beverage business, and who could integrate its various facets into one efficient operation. Steele was someone ready and able to make the tough decisions necessary to save Pepsi-Cola.

To say things looked grim for Pepsi-Cola when Steele took the helm would be an understatement. Through much of 1949, Pepsi-Cola

teetered on the brink of bankruptcy. By the time Steele took over as president in 1950, his former colleagues in Atlanta smugly agreed that he was presiding over the dismantling of their competitor. In fact, the majority of the investment community was betting Pepsi-Cola would be out of business by 1951.

Of the myriad problems facing Steele, the most serious was the severe decline in sales of Pepsi-Cola. For the company to survive, this downward spiral, begun in 1947, would have to stop immediately. Steele's challenge was to convince Pepsi bottlers as well as the public and business community that Pepsi-Cola remained a viable company, eager to win the battle to be the consumers' drink of choice.

To dramatically improve sales, what was needed was a full-scale aggressive advertising campaign—one ambitious enough not only to increase public awareness of the product but also to state loud and clear that Pepsi-Cola was a prime contender in the cola market.

In tune with the postwar economic expansion that relegated economy secondary to image, Pepsi's new slogan, MORE BOUNCE TO THE OUNCE, was distinctly upbeat—and devoid of any mention of value. Along the same lines, new ads featured people having the time of their lives while drinking a Pepsi-Cola.

The new advertising campaign consisted of a three-pronged approach. First, a considerable amount of money was spent on television advertising. Given that TV was a novelty at the time, Pepsi-Cola

**106**

# Metal Crown Tacker M-168

One of the most popular signs in our metal line. Easy to handle... takes a minute to put up. Use at baseball parks, stadiums, booths in fairs, fruit and vegetable markets, groceries, food stores, delicatessens, roadside stands, filling stations, tourist camps, boat houses, fishing and hunting clubs.

**M-168   Metal Crown Tacker**

**Size:**      31″ wide x 27″ high.

**Colors:**   Full color on white background.

**Material:**  30-gauge steel, folded edges, 8 holes punched in border for tacking.

**Price:**     $21.25 per case of 25, weighing 40 lbs., f.o.b. St. Louis, Mo.

**CHARGEABLE TO BOTTLE POINT-OF-PURCHASE FUND**
*Please specify preferred method of shipping and routing.*
Order form included in back of this catalog.

---

# 64 Carton Display Stand

## CS-64 Bin Type Design — For Volume Outlets — Easily Assembled

**CS-64 Carton Display Stand**

**Specifications**

| | |
|---|---|
| **Capacity:** | 64 Cartons |
| **Packaged:** | 2 Per Carton |
| **Dimensions:** | 26″ x 33″ x 60″ high (Includes Sign) |
| **Shipping Weight:** | 79 Lbs. Per Carton |
| **Finish:** | Baked Vinyl Aluminum |
| **Price:** | $11.10 Each (Includes Sign) |
| **Minimum Order:** | One Carton (2 Stands) |
| **Sign:** | Masonite Silk Screened on Both Sides |
| **Order From:** | Bottler's Order Dept. |

**D.S.4 Masonite Sign**
(For CS-64 Display Stand)

| | |
|---|---|
| **Packaged:** | 4 Per Carton |
| **Finish:** | Silk Screened on Both Sides |
| **Price:** | $1.30 each ($5.20 Per Carton of 4) |
| **Minimum Order:** | One Carton |
| **Order From:** | Bottler's Order Dept. |

**CHARGEABLE TO BOTTLE POINT-OF-PURCHASE FUND**
*(Prices Subject to Change Without Notice)*

*In the 1950s, Pepsi-Cola advertising evolved from chaotic to thematic.*

*Pepsi developed a strong take-home business in the early 1940s, which continued into the 1950s.*

PRODUCTS
RESHING·SATISFYING
BIGGER·BETTER
5¢
3659
Dossin's
Miss Pepsi V
Pepsi-Cola

*Even while the Pepsi-*

*Cola Company was*

*struggling in the early*

*1950s, some of their*

*bottlers were doing quite*

*well. The Dossin family*

*of Detroit, Michigan,*

*sponsored a racing boat.*

MORE BOUNCE TO THE OUNCE advertising combined product benefit and lifestyle. For the first time in their history, Pepsi-Cola was offering a consistent advertising program.

Right: "The Faye Emerson Show," which aired in 1950 and starred one of early television's most popular personalities, was Pepsi's first effort to sponsor a weekly television program.

Pepsi promoted "The Faye Emerson Show" in their magazine ads.

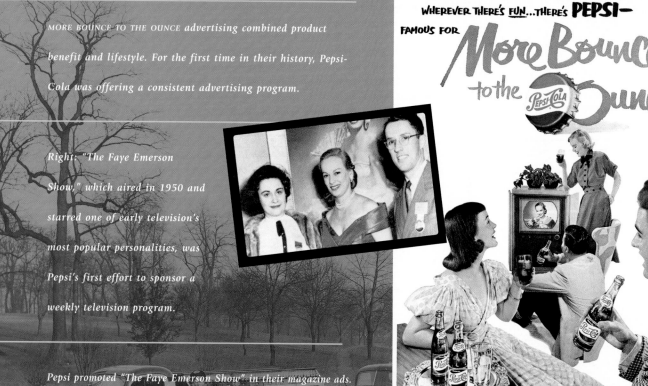

boldly pioneered its use as a way to advertise a national brand. People were utterly fascinated by television—anything at all that appeared on its screen intrigued the viewer. The company shrewdly gambled that by advertising on TV, Pepsi would be linked in the public mind to the modern American lifestyle.

Pepsi-Cola debuted on TV with its sponsorship of "The Faye Emerson Program," ensuring a large viewing audience. Emerson, honored by *Look* magazine as TV's most appealing personality, was considered the First Lady of television.

Pepsi-Cola soon discovered that one bonus of advertising on television was that audiences had a habit of snacking while viewing. Pepsi-Cola had a way of bolstering their success in the take-home market, as the televised ads reinforced Pepsi's image as the television-viewing public's soft drink of choice.

The second prong of Pepsi-Cola's advertising strategy was radio ads. The Pepsi-Cola jingle had already made the product a household name—Pepsi-Cola radio spots would now associate that name with quality.

Beginning in 1950, Pepsi-Cola sponsored a twice-weekly radio program called "Counter Spy," a high-quality suspense thriller attuned to the postwar mood of geopolitical intrigue. With a nod to authority and a salute to patriotism, the company's commercial relayed the official sanction of the United States Testing Company Inc., proclaiming that Pepsi-Cola had been tested and found to have the highest purity and more quick food energy and value ounce for ounce than all other leading nationally known cola drinks.

Riding the national wave of patriotism through the Korean War, Pepsi-Cola sponsored "The Phil Regan Armed Services Show," premiering on March 4, 1951. Broadcast on network radio stations nationwide as it toured military installations across the United States, the program's variety show format was hosted by cop-turned-entertainer Regan, known as the singing policeman.

Pepsi-Cola's third advertising strategy involved print media. Ads were featured in many leading national magazines, including *Life, Look,* and *The Saturday Evening Post.* The ads depicted people enjoying life to the full—including a full glass of Pepsi. Prominently displayed was the slogan MORE BOUNCE TO THE OUNCE, along with the tag line WHY TAKE LESS—WHEN PEPSI'S BEST! Taking advantage of the opportunity to cross promote, the ads reminded readers to watch "The Faye Emerson Show" on television and tune into "The Phil Regan Armed Services Show" on radio.

Steele faced the problem of how to fund this ambitious advertising campaign. Assets were promptly put up for sale. Early in 1950, Pepsi-Cola was paid $4 million for its Cuban sugar plantation, which had never really provided a steady supply of affordable sugar. Also sold was Pepsi-Cola's bottle cap manufacturing facility at the Long Island City plant—the company discovered that it was more cost-effective to buy caps from established suppliers.

Meanwhile, the advertising strategy was justifying its substantial price tag. By October 1950, sales began to rebound. By January and February of 1951, sales rose 15 percent over the previous year. Steele and his team were evidently setting Pepsi-Cola on the right course.

When Steele took over in 1950, he believed that many key managers lacked the skills and experience necessary to reverse the company's dwindling fortunes. He

*The majority of Pepsi-Cola's advertising during the '50s was targeted at the cold bottle and take-home markets.*

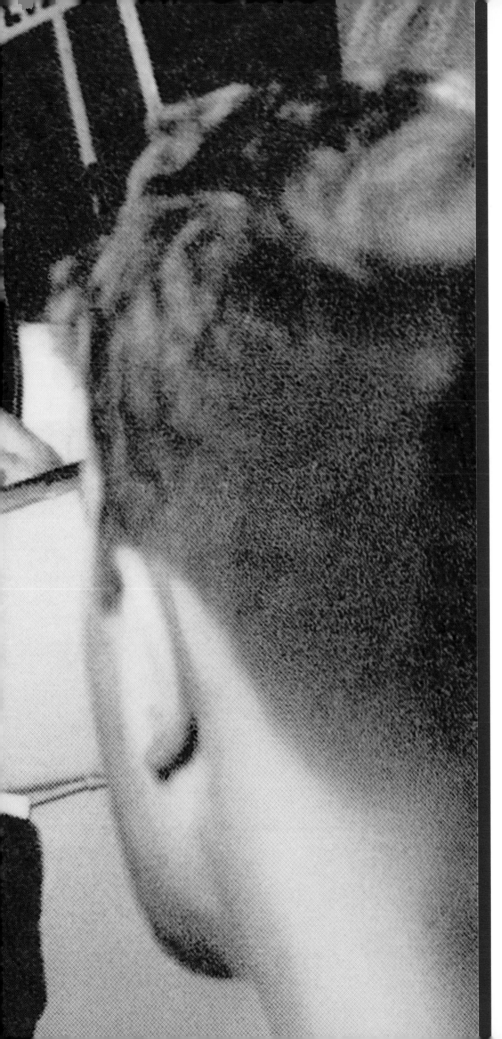

*Attractive in-store displays enticed*

*retailers to display Pepsi-Cola.*

didn't hesitate to recruit from other soft drink companies, and soon assembled a crackerjack team equipped to meet the challenges facing the Pepsi-Cola Company.

Besides bringing on board qualified management, Steele introduced a working philosophy that the bottler played an essential role in Pepsi-Cola's success. No matter how much the company advertised, if bottlers failed to persuade local retailers to carry Pepsi-Cola, the product wouldn't be bought. Large-scale advertising may have made Pepsi-Cola popular, but it was the day-to-day work of the bottlers and their employees that actually sold Pepsi-Cola.

*Photographing leaders such as President Truman*

*with a Pepsi in hand was an excellent way to*

*get free advertising.*

*Pepsi-Cola strove to be associated with popular images of the American lifestyle.*

*Improved advertising and marketing helped restore the confidence of Pepsi bottlers in the parent company.*

Stories are told of the proverbial frantic phone call to the local Pepsi-Cola bottler from an out-of-stock retailer. Whatever the hour of day or night, the bottler would drive to the plant, pick up the requisite number of cases of Pepsi-Cola, and deliver them personally to the retailer. Efforts like this built loyal customers in a way that advertising never could.

Under Steele's leadership, a new spirit of cooperation developed between the local bottler and the parent company. It was understood that the bottler and the company were equal partners—that success for the Pepsi-Cola Company could only be realized when the bottler succeeded. Above all, the bottler was expected to be treated with respect.

Steele's approach repaired a rift between local bottlers and the parent company that had been growing over the years. The parent company's insistence on continuing to offer the 12-ounce bottle for a nickel despite slipping profits seriously damaged the relationship with the bottlers, who chafed at what they felt was the company's insensitivity to their problems. Such actions had perpetuated the bottlers' general lack of confidence in the Pepsi-Cola Company; the bottlers, in turn, cut back in their efforts to promote Pepsi-Cola.

Compounding the problem, communication between the bottlers and the parent company in New York via territory representatives had broken down.

More and more, it seemed that New York dictated policy after policy without concern for how the bottlers might be affected. As a result, the bottlers felt increasingly isolated from the management of the Pepsi-Cola Company.

Convinced that success in the soft drink business depended on a network of motivated and dedicated bottlers, Steele opened up direct lines of communication between the head office and the bottlers. Territory representatives were replaced by a national system of regional offices designed to bring the policy makers in closer contact with the bottlers, facilitating feedback from the bottlers, who, after all, faced the consequences of those policies.

**114**

Reinvigorating both advertising and bottler relations was only part of Steele's plan to revive Pepsi-Cola. Improving quality control was also on his agenda. With more than 400 independent Pepsi-Cola bottlers producing the cola drink, maintaining consistency in flavor and taste posed a formidable task.

Letters flooded Pepsi-Cola, complaining that the beverage was too sweet, too tart, too carbonated, or not carbonated enough. Careless production or personnel or faulty equipment could easily alter the flavor of Pepsi-Cola. Past controls had required bottlers to send samples to the New York facility to be tested. This system, however, proved ineffective, as months would sometimes pass before notification was received that a bottler's Pepsi-Cola did not meet company standards.

Pepsi-Cola reversed this process, sending out mobile laboratories from bottler to bottler, testing the Pepsi-Cola produced at each plant. Once a lab technician had conducted an evaluation of the product, a bottler might receive instruction on how to bring the beverage into compliance with company standards. This efficient method of correcting any deviance in standards ensured the consistent quality of Pepsi-Cola. And the company made direct reference to the mobile laboratories in its ads, touting Pepsi-Cola as a product of the highest quality standards.

Steele's program to improve Pepsi-Cola's image involved modernizing all plants and machinery. In line with this strategy, the script trademark that had been used since 1909 was redesigned to give it a more modern look.

The equipment used to print directly on bottles had been developed during World War II. At war's end, the move was on to switch from paper labels to applied labels, thus sprucing up the look of Pepsi-Cola. But bottlers made this change only halfheartedly, as it cost them a pretty penny. By the early 1950s, huge quantities of Pepsi-Cola bottles with paper labels were still being sold.

Besides their shabby appearance, the paper-label bottles were unpopular with retailers because such bottles invariably shed their labels in water coolers. Steele eventually intervened and decreed it a policy that only applied color labels appear on bottles of Pepsi-Cola.

Another of Steele's beliefs was that in order to achieve success, Pepsi-Cola must penetrate all existing soft drink markets. To accomplish this, he adopted a two-bottle strategy. First, with the

*The image of Pepsi-Cola was enhanced by attractive new bottles and eye-catching ads.*

*This thermometer not only told the public how hot it was, but also reminded people that one antidote to the heat was a cool drink of Pepsi-Cola.*

*Alfred Steele understood that for Pepsi-Cola to succeed, the company would need committed bottlers.*

PEPSI COLA CONVENTION

CHICAGO, ILLINOIS—JANUARY—1951

The Pepsi-Cola Company and its 650 bottlers are dedicated to the idea of making Pepsi-Cola the most wholesome refreshment you can buy.

To bring this ideal to reality, Pepsi-Cola not only exercises the greatest care in its own laboratories—but has developed its field laboratory which goes from one bottling plant to another, helping your Pepsi-Cola bottler meet Pepsi-Cola standards of quality.

This mobile laboratory checks every detail starting with the water supply—which may be good enough to drink yet not be good enough for the delicate flavor of Pepsi-Cola. From there the laboratory checks sugar, concentrate, syrup, cleansing agents, bottles, crowns—every step involved in bringing Pepsi-Cola to your mouth.

There is now a fleet of these field laboratories in operation all over the country. When it comes to what you drink no standard is too high, no care too great.

The mobile lab is but one example of the spirit of cooperation that exists between Pepsi-Cola and its bottlers.

This exchange of know-how may not show up on our financial sheet. But it is one of our greatest assets, and a very real factor in the large sales increases of Pepsi-Cola in recent years. Have a Pepsi.®

**The Quality of Pepsi-Cola* is no accident**

*Pepsi-Cola Company*
3 West 57th Street, New York

*Pepsi-Cola is the product of Pepsi-Cola Company—bottled by authorized bottlers all over the world.

*A priority in the early 1950s was making the taste of Pepsi-Cola consistent from coast to coast.*

12-ounce bottle (10 ounces in some areas), he expanded the take-home business that had long been Pepsi-Cola's strongest market. Second, an eight-ounce bottle was promoted as an on-premises drink to be sold in vending machines, at movie theaters and sporting events, and even on airlines.

The vending machine market offered the greatest opportunity for Pepsi-Cola. To encourage bottlers to invest in vending machines, Steele arranged easy financing and low interest rates for bottlers who purchased them. Overnight, Pepsi-Cola vending machines began popping up everywhere, especially at gasoline stations.

With more Americans owning auto-

mobiles and taking them on the road for family vacations, service stations appeared as oases along the nation's highways. What better than a cool refreshing Pepsi-Cola while your gas tank was being filled on a sweltering summer day?

Many Pepsi-Cola bottlers stocked a flat-top vending machine that held a variety of bottled soft drinks—quite generous, given Coca-Cola's penchant for offering only their own beverage in their machines. A customer would lift the top, drop a coin in the slot, pick out his or her flavor of choice, and slide the bottle along a rail to the opening of the machine, where the bottle would be released into his or her hands.

Steele's innovations were paying off. Pepsi-Cola was moving well beyond the goal of mere survival. Indeed, Steele's sights were set squarely on defeating Coca-Cola. The battle cry around Pepsi-Cola was now "Beat Coke." A natural leader and motivator, Steele made his employees believe that this—and even more—was possible.

Nineteen fifty was a landmark year, marking not only the beginning of the second half of the 20th century but also the beginning of a new technological age. Jet planes, televisions, and even computers would soon become part of everyday life in America.

In the early 1950s, consumer testing revealed a trend for foods that were less heavy and less sweet. In the tough times of the Great Depression, people had counted on getting the maximum energy and calories from the food that they consumed. In the prosperous 1950s, more taste with fewer calories became the ideal.

To meet consumer demand for lighter foods, Pepsi-Cola's Long Island City laboratory was directed to reformulate Pepsi-Cola.

By 1953, a lighter-tasting Pepsi was developed containing less sugar. To promote the new taste, the company introduced a new advertising slogan—THE LIGHT REFRESHMENT.

Beginning in 1953, THE LIGHT REFRESHMENT campaign took Pepsi-Cola advertising in a new direction. To take advantage of the transformation of America into a society shaping the modern age, Pepsi-Cola positioned itself as the drink of the modern generation. The new ads featured people wearing the latest fashions and up-to-the-minute hairstyles, all enjoying the best that the 1950s had to offer, including, of course, Pepsi-Cola.

These ads were calculated to promote Pepsi-Cola as the soft drink that made life enjoyable—distancing it from previous advertising that emphasized affordability. The damage to the product's reputation from the older ads had become a sore spot for Pepsi-Cola. It was whispered that when entertaining at home, people sometimes poured Pepsi-Cola into glasses in their kitchens, out of sight of their guests seated in the living room. By 1953, the situation had changed to the point that Pepsi-Cola was proudly served not only at home, but also in public venues across the country.

Pepsi-Cola's modern image was enhanced by a successful series of radio and television commercials featuring film star Polly Bergen. A highlight of these commercials was an updated version of the Pepsi-Cola jingle sung by Bergen. Bergen proved to be a charming and enthusiastic ambassador for Pepsi-Cola, making personal

*Vending machines allowed Pepsi-Cola to expand the places where the drink could be sold. Pepsi-Cola used different styles of vending machines in different locations.*

The Light refreshment

FOSTER and KLEISER

Steele believed that you couldn't save your
way to prosperity, so he spent huge amounts
of money on advertising and expansion.

# Have a Pepsi

## Pepsi-Cola
refreshes without filling

Today's pace is for the

*Slender*

THE LIGHT REFRESHMENT *advertising campaign*

*capitalized on consumer demand for food*

*products containing fewer calories.*

*Pepsi's former image as an economy drink was*

*replaced by* THE LIGHT REFRESHMENT *ads.*

Times Square at Night, New York City

135

90760

*In 1955, Pepsi-Cola built the world's largest advertising display in New York City's Times Square.*

*Popular actress Polly Bergen became Pepsi-Cola's first celebrity spokesperson. She traveled around the country, promoting the soft drink.*

appearances around the country. In fact, she was even called Miss Pepsi-Cola.

The light refreshment ad campaign would transform all displays of Pepsi-Cola, from vending machines to fountain dispensers. Lighter, brighter colors were achieving a more appealing uniform appearance. Pepsi-Cola was becoming a modern soft drink company.

Steele had a reputation for showmanship. He thrived on producing extravaganzas to attract publicity. In 1955, he achieved two spectacular events for Pepsi-Cola—the world's largest display in Times Square and Pepsi-Cola's debut at Disneyland.

The Times Square electric sign made its debut in April 1955. Two 50-foot porcelain Pepsi-Cola bottle signs and a 50-foot bottle cap were illuminated with 35,000 lights and more than a mile of neon tubing. If that weren't enough, a 50,000-gallon waterfall flowed under the bottle cap, down the 45 feet between the two bottle signs. A major attraction in Times Square—which itself draws immense crowds—the lighted Pepsi-Cola sign has appeared on innumerable postcards as well as on the movie screen.

Also garnering enormous publicity for Pepsi-Cola in 1955, the soft drink became the featured beverage in an attraction at the new theme park in Anaheim, California, built by Walt Disney. This agreement had its start a year earlier, when Edward Specht, Pepsi-Cola's national accounts representative in Los Angeles, heard that cartoon czar Disney was developing an amusement park. After making inquiries at Disney's Burbank studios and seeing the blueprints himself, Specht immediately contacted Pepsi headquarters.

*The 26-ounce "hostess" bottle was Pepsi's first large bottle.*

*To emphasize Pepsi-Cola's new lighter image, the predominant color of most advertising was changed to yellow.*

In response, Donald Kendall, vice president of national accounts, was dispatched to meet with C.V. Wood, general manager of Disneyland. The result was a financial commitment making Pepsi-Cola one of the first national companies to sign a Disneyland contract.

When Disneyland opened on July 18, 1955, Pepsi-Cola was there—in Slue-Foot Sue's Golden Horseshoe Revue. Slue-Foot Sue's was a 19th century–inspired opera house in which musicians performed

Pepsi used THE LIGHT REFRESHMENT *ad campaign when sponsoring such television events as* Annie Get Your Gun *and* Cinderella. *Commercials aired during* Annie Get Your Gun *featured legendary comedian Harpo Marx.*

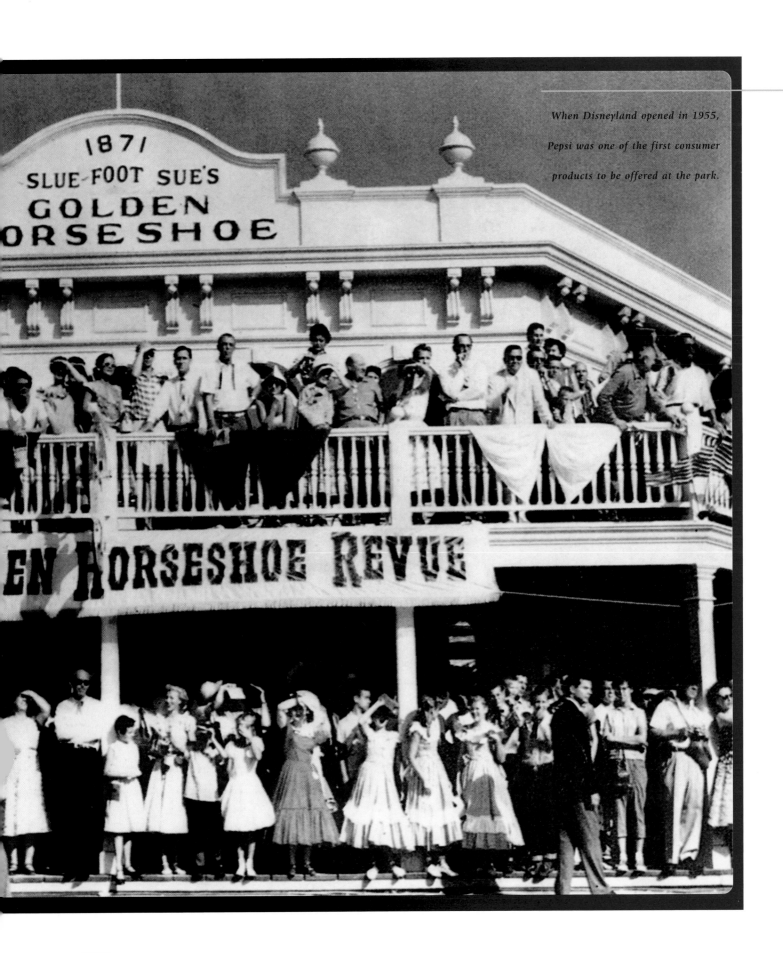

When Disneyland opened in 1955, Pepsi was one of the first consumer products to be offered at the park.

*One of Pepsi-Cola's largest promotions was sponsorship of the Miss America Pageant, which began in the 1950s.*

*In 1955, Alfred Steele, president of the Pepsi-Cola Company, married Oscar-winning film star Joan Crawford. The Steeles promoted Pepsi all over the world.*

nostalgic tunes. Saloon patrons were served Pepsi-Cola.

Appearing with Walt Disney when Slue-Foot Sue's opened its doors was Kendall. Many people contributed to Pepsi-Cola's presence at the grand opening of the Magic Kingdom, but Kendall was foremost in making it happen. For this and other accomplishments, Kendall was made president of Pepsi-Cola International in 1957.

Another successful Pepsi-Cola sponsorship was the 1957 CBS showing of *Cinderella*, the debut of a Richard Rodgers and Oscar Hammerstein musical on television. Costarring with Broadway's Julie Andrews was Jon Cypher as Prince Charming, who, upon leaving the live broadcast, found Manhattan's Upper West Side devoid of pedestrians and cabs, resembling "a post-nuclear disaster." Everyone had been inside, in front of their TVs. With an estimated 107 million people watching, *Cinderella* broke all records for the viewing of a single TV program.

*Cinderella*'s success led to Pepsi-Cola sponsorship of another special, *Annie Get Your Gun*, starring Mary Martin—another Broadway star—airing on Thanksgiving eve, 1957. The Pepsi commercials that night were almost as entertaining as the program—one featured the irrepressible Harpo Marx. An estimated 65 million people watched the broadcast, giving Pepsi-Cola another television success.

In another great promotional move, Pepsi-Cola sponsored the 1958 Miss America pageant. This enabled bottlers to get involved at the local and state pageants leading up to the national event in Atlantic City. And the publicity didn't end there. Whoever ended up being crowned Miss America would appear at events nationwide on behalf of Pepsi-Cola. The relationship between Pepsi-Cola and the Miss America pageant would last nearly a decade.

In 1955, James Carkner, one of the final holdovers from the Loft management, stepped down as chairman of the board of the Pepsi-Cola Company. Steele promptly assumed the chairmanship, gaining control over Pepsi-Cola's international as well as domestic operations.

With Steele as chairman of the board, Herbert L. Barnet assumed the presidency of the Pepsi-Cola Company. Barnet's association with Pepsi-Cola began when he had worked as a young lawyer for the firm representing Loft in its lawsuit against Guth. In 1949, Barnet was persuaded to abandon the law to join Pepsi-Cola's management team. He started out as vice president of national accounts. In 1950, he was promoted to vice president of domestic operations, a position he held until he became president.

In 1955, Steele married movie star Joan Crawford, who became part of the Pepsi-Cola family. She appeared prominently at Steele's side as he traveled the world conducting business. As one reporter put it, normally a few hundred people appeared at a Pepsi-Cola plant opening but when Crawford accompanied her husband to an opening, 50,000 onlookers and hundreds of journalists showed up. Crawford had a featured role in these openings—as the one who cut the ribbon.

After Steele's death in 1959, Crawford continued her association with Pepsi-Cola, serving as a member of the board and as a goodwill ambassador. Her service with the company continued until 1974.

THE LIGHT REFRESHMENT advertising theme worked well for Pepsi-Cola from 1953 to 1957. During those years, as public perception of Pepsi-Cola improved, sales and profits skyrocketed. But after five years, it was time for something new. In 1958, the Kenyon and Eckhardt ad agency, hired by Pepsi-Cola two years earlier, introduced the BE SOCIABLE, HAVE A PEPSI campaign, along with the first new Pepsi theme song in nearly 20 years.

The original Pepsi-Cola jingle, which had debuted in 1939, was used in various incarnations until 1957, with new words having been put to the old tune in 1951. But now, even with the new lyrics, the jingle sounded outdated.

The new "Pepsi-Cola Refreshment Song," which debuted in 1958, would be heard thousands of times on television and radio. This new theme song was closely tied to the BE SOCIABLE slogan.

The modernization of Pepsi-Cola also entailed a more eye-catching bottle. This new design had been created in the early 1950s by Max Lomont, art director of Pepsi-Cola, who introduced a family of bottles with a swirl design. In 1958, this design expanded from 26- and 6.5-ounce bottles to include 10- and 12-ounce bottles.

*By the end of 1959, Pepsi-Cola's business had increased so much that bigger delivery trucks were needed.*

*The* LIGHT REFRESHMENT

*advertising campaign*

*gradually evolved into*

*one using the slogan*

BE SOCIABLE.

*The* BE SOCIABLE

*advertising campaign*

*ran from 1959 to 1960.*

The makeover that Pepsi-Cola had undergone in the 1950s was just about complete. What was left? The name Pepsi-Cola itself. Many of the company's marketing people believed that a shorter name would be easier to say and sound friendlier to consumers.

So the SAY PEPSI, PLEASE campaign was launched. The challenge was to reprogram consumers to replace Pepsi-Cola with simply Pepsi. Based on the theory that people liked to win prizes and were fascinated by the novelty of hearing their own voices, the company set up recording booths around the towns targeted for the promotion. Passers-by were invited to stop at the booths and record the line *Pepsi, please!*

A number of these recorded voices were then played on the radio. The first person to identify his or her own voice won a prize.

The promotion was a huge success.

People everywhere were reciting "Pepsi, please!" Gradually, the word *cola* disappeared from the company's advertising and logo. As evidence of the success of the campaign, today it would sound odd to hear someone ask for a Pepsi-Cola.

Meanwhile, a large contingent at Pepsi-Cola lobbied for the company to offer other products besides Pepsi. Research indicated that consumers wanted a variety of soft drink flavors—especially lemon-lime. Responding to consumer demand, in 1959 Pepsi-Cola introduced Teem, a lemon-lime drink that the company was confident could be sold alongside Pepsi without hurting Pepsi sales. Introduced locally to keep advertising costs down, the drink was announced with the slogan NEW TEEM IS IN TOWN.

The 1950s have the distinction of being the greatest period of growth and expansion in the history of the Pepsi-Cola

Company. Under Steele's leadership, the company was forged into a modern unified soft drink corporation. By the end of 1959, sales had soared to more than $157 million.

Over the decade, more than 200 new Pepsi-Cola bottling plants were built. Moreover, the number of plants selling more than a million cases of Pepsi-Cola a year jumped from 15 in 1950 to 70 by 1959. A lot of Pepsi-Cola was being rung up at store cash registers. Indeed, in nine years, sales increased by a whopping 184 percent.

Such increases were not limited to domestic business. International operations experienced such tremendous growth that in April 1954 the export department set up by Guth to handle international franchises and sales was superseded by Pepsi-Cola International Ltd. Instead of being merely a division of the Pepsi-Cola

Company, overseas operations had graduated to subsidiary status.

In fact, from 1950 to 1959, international sales increased nearly five times. Over the same period, 200 new plants opened outside the United States. Pepsi-Cola was now available in 80 countries, representing 300 million people.

The architect of Pepsi-Cola's success in the 1950s, Alfred Steele, died near the decade's end. In April 1959, while traveling the country promoting Pepsi-Cola, he suffered a heart attack.

In the final days of 1959, the Pepsi-Cola Company moved into its new home at 500 Park Avenue in New York City. This new location symbolized Pepsi-Cola's rise in the soft drink business, for on Park Avenue, the company shared an address with America's most prestigious corporations.

*"The Pepsi-Cola Refreshment Song" was the drink's first new jingle since 1939.*

*Pepsi-Cola introduced the swirl bottle in 1958.*

*In 1959, Pepsi-Cola International president Don Kendall encouraged Nixon and Khrushchev to "Be Sociable."*

# "cold warriors" learn to be sociable

One of Pepsi's most significant events, arranged by Pepsi-Cola International president Don Kendall, occurred at the 1959 American Exposition in Moscow, an international event in which Coca-Cola had declined to participate. It was the height of the Cold War, when the United States and the Soviet Union were engaged in a conflict marked by rivalry and mistrust.

The night before the exposition opened, Kendall attended a reception held for Vice President Richard M. Nixon at the U.S. Embassy, where he confided to Nixon that his job was in jeopardy and he needed Khrushchev to visit the Pepsi-Cola kiosk. Nixon agreed to bring the Soviet premier by the following day.

When Nixon and Khrushchev stopped by the Pepsi booth, Kendall quickly maneuvered a Pepsi into each of their hands. Of course, the world press was there to snap the picture while the two leaders sipped their Pepsis. Referring to Pepsi-Cola's slogan BE SOCIABLE, HAVE A PEPSI, the headline in the Philadelphia Inquirer read KHRUSHCHEV LEARNS TO BE SOCIABLE.

This headline and many like it were emblazoned on newspapers the world over. The publicity may well have helped propel Kendall to the presidency of Pepsi-Cola.

Have a Pepsi

# come alive! you're in the pepsi generation

Pepsi-Cola had begun the 1950s not knowing if the company would survive a year, let alone a decade. But by 1960, Pepsi-Cola was in the best financial shape ever. Sales had increased from just under $24 million in 1950 to over $157 million by 1960.

Pepsi-Cola had managed to convince consumers that its soft drink was more than just a bargain cola. In fact, Pepsi-Cola was now the world's second leading soft drink. The company, infused with confidence, was poised to make its product the number one cola drink.

To emerge as the leader in the industry, Pepsi-Cola would have to be on the cutting edge of societal change. Pepsi's growth over the previous decade owed as much to innovation and hard work as to Coke's resistance to change. And change would touch every aspect of society in the 1960s. The 1960s, a decade of upheaval, brought about major changes in the way people purchased soft drinks as well as in the way companies advertised them. Pepsi's success in the 1960s was due in part to the company's willingness to take risks, adopt new marketing techniques, and adapt to change.

The old way of doing things was being swept away by modern, more convenient methods. Mom-and-pop stores—where, prior to the 1960s, most bottled soft drinks were sold—were being replaced by gleaming new supermarkets. In one New York City neighborhood alone, 120 family stores were replaced by three supermarkets.

Pepsi's earlier experimentation with cans and no-return bottles took root in the 1960s.

*Through hard-hitting promotion and innovative advertising, by 1960 Pepsi had established a reputation as the modern American soft drink.*

*The* NOW IT'S PEPSI— FOR THOSE WHO THINK YOUNG *campaign was the company's first ad aimed entirely at lifestyle.*

*By 1960, consumer*

*demand for Pepsi had*

*been on the increase for*

*nine straight years.*

The revenue from strong sales allowed Pepsi to present the highest quality of advertising in the company's history.

Pepsi reintroduced canned cola in 1960. The company's initial foray into this market in 1949 was unsuccessful.

"Wagon Train" was one of the many popular television programs sponsored by Pepsi in the 1960s.

These stills from a THINK YOUNG commercial show the primitive style of 1962 television advertising.

# NEW! PEPSI HALF-QUARTS

# now it's Pepsi
## for those who think young

Always a packaging innovator, Pepsi introduced the 16-ounce bottle in 1960.

The slogan THINK YOUNG was pasted on roadside billboards and painted on the sides of buildings. Soon everyone was thinking young—and drinking Pepsi.

*Pepsi-Cola's sponsorship of the Miss America Pageant provided hundreds of scholarships for young women.*

*Pepsi-Cola bottlers had spent millions modernizing plants and building new ones in the 1950s, and were ready to compete for leadership in the cola market.*

Cans had been a rarity throughout the 1950s. But improved technology that ensured better flavor, along with increased demand by consumers, caused cans to become a prime factor in sales. By 1965, 3.8 billion soft drinks were sold in cans worldwide. In fact, cans represented almost 12 percent of the packaged soft drinks sold in the United States that year.

For the Pepsi bottler, cans provided an opportunity to increase sales; however, the expense of adding a canning line to most bottling plants was prohibitive. But not for long—innovative Pepsi bottlers formed canning cooperatives. These cooperatives were successful, and many are still operating today.

During the economic boom of the 1950s, many companies grew complacent. But Pepsi didn't let up—especially because the company believed that it had a good chance of gaining the number one spot. Equipped with a potent advertising program and the latest marketing techniques, Pepsi sought to unseat Coca-Cola as the industry leader.

Pepsi's marketing and advertising plans for the 1960s were more aggressive than ever. After learning that demographers had identified the babies born after World War II as an important market for consumer products in the 1960s, Pepsi promptly hired a new advertising agency. Batton, Barton, Durstire, and Osborn, known as BBDO, would remain Pepsi's principal advertising agency for the next 30 years. BBDO created advertising aimed directly at baby boomers—as this emerging market was called. Pepsi even claimed these youth as their own, telling them that Pepsi was their drink of choice.

BBDO's first offering, the NOW IT'S PEPSI—FOR THOSE WHO THINK YOUNG campaign, featured a bright new Pepsi song. Written to the tune of Walter Donaldson and Gus Kahn's jaunty roaring '20s ballad "Makin' Whoopee," it was performed by pert recording star Joannie Sommers in commercials airing on radio and TV. To reinforce this message, magazine ads mirrored the youthful images of the TV commercials. Pepsi commercials appeared on a series featuring Hollywood musical star Jane Powell, as well as on such quintessential shows of the era as "Aquanauts," "Laramie," "Cheyenne," and "The Asphalt Jungle."

The NOW IT'S PEPSI—FOR THOSE WHO THINK YOUNG ad campaign was so successful that by 1962, 64 percent of the U.S. population could identify the theme as Pepsi's. That same year, Pepsi commercials reached viewers of the most popular television shows of the era, including "Wagon Train," "Ben Casey", and "The Twilight Zone."

Advertising wasn't the only thing changing at Pepsi. Company researchers had discovered a number of small companies having success with a 16-ounce bottle. Recalling how Pepsi's rebirth had resulted from offering a larger bottle than its competitors—the cola giant from Atlanta reluctantly sold its product in 12-ounce bottles—the company began to test-market a 16-ounce bottle. The tests proved positive, so Pepsi marketed the larger bottle, beginning in 1960.

The Pepsi bottler in Billings, Montana,

credited the success of the 16-ounce bottle to Pepsi's domination of the soft drink market. The residents of Billings took to the large Pepsi bottle so quickly that employees at the Billings bottling plant were forced to speed up production to meet the demand. This story was repeated over and over as America's taste for cola drinks increased, evidenced by the number of bottles consumed by one person in a year.

With assorted packaging, including the new 16-ounce bottle, Pepsi planned to expand its consumer base. In 1960, the company test-marketed the no deposit–no return bottle. In addition, after a nine-year hiatus, Pepsi again became available in cans. And to keep up with consumer demand for more convenient packaging, Pepsi-Cola began offering an eight-bottle carton. As another way of increasing market share, Pepsi-Cola in 1960 introduced Patio, a line of flavored drinks, including orange, grape, root beer, and ginger ale.

*Pepsi believed that nonreturnable bottles would become an integral part of the soft drink business.*

*Don Kendall, who began his career as a fountain syrup salesman in 1947, became president of Pepsi-Cola in 1963.*

come alive!

## You're in the Pepsi generation!

This is the liveliest, most energetic time ever...with the most active generation living it. You're part of it. Pepsi-Cola is part, too. Pepsi is the modern, light refreshment...with that bold, clean taste and energy to liven your pace. It's the official drink of everyone with a thirst for living!

"PEPSI-COLA" AND "PEPSI" ARE TRADEMARKS OF PEPSI-COLA COMPANY, REG. U.S. PAT. OFF. © 1964, PEPSI-COLA COMPANY

*The PEPSI GENERATION advertising—directed at baby boomers—hit the bull's-eye.*

*In an effort to modernize its image, Pepsi abandoned its script logo for a more contemporary logo in 1963.*

In 1963, after years of research, Patio Diet Cola appeared on grocery store shelves. A youth-oriented American public, more conscious of physical fitness and personal appearance, became interested in dietetic beverages. Pepsi's initial attempt at a low-calorie artificially sweetened cola drink did not do well. Undeterred, the company persisted in developing a successful diet cola.

That same year, in a continuing effort to be perceived as modern, Pepsi replaced its script logo with one featuring the Pepsi name in block letters across a stylized bot-

tle cap. This design had the "pop art" look that had become the rage, from New York galleries to the "Batman" TV show.

Also in 1963, Pepsi-Cola had a new president. After eight years, Herbert Barnet vacated the presidency to become chairman of the board of Pepsi-Cola. Barnet provided steady leadership during the chaotic period following Steele's unexpected death. With sales weakening and the parent company increasing the price of concentrate, the bottlers were looking for new leadership. In what appeared to be a mini revolt, the bottlers went to the board, requesting a new president. The board selected Kendall, hoping that he could revitalize the domestic operations in the same way that he had revitalized Pepsi's overseas business.

Kendall's career with Pepsi-Cola had begun in 1947, when Mack hired him as a syrup salesman for the New York area. Kendall rapidly rose through the ranks. By 1948, he was a fountain sales manager in the New York area; a year later, he was the fountain sales manager for the entire company. By 1952, he was vice president and head of the national accounts department, where he distinguished himself by signing hundreds of new national accounts for Pepsi, including Disneyland. Then, in 1963, Kendall took on the presidency of Pepsi-Cola—in just 16 years, he had worked his way up from salesman to president of the company.

One of Kendall's challenges was to lead Pepsi in following up the success of the THINK YOUNG campaign with something just as effective. In the fall of 1963, Pepsi-Cola unveiled the COME ALIVE, YOU'RE IN THE PEPSI GENERATION campaign. Tapping into the growing number of Pepsi drinkers among the baby boomers, Pepsi dubbed this group the Pepsi Generation and targeted ads to their buoyant energetic spirit. Pulling out all the stops to reach these 25 million or so "boomers," Pepsi bought 85 percent more television coverage than for their previous campaign.

Heralding the COME ALIVE campaign, a two-minute commercial appeared during the Miss America pageant telecast in September 1963, to an estimated 60 million American viewers. Featured in this first color commercial from Pepsi-Cola was a song built around the new theme. And, breaking new ground, the company's new Diet Pepsi was advertised alongside Pepsi.

After disappointing sales of Patio Diet Cola, Pepsi-Cola decided to withdraw the product in favor of Diet Pepsi. This unprecedented marketing decision—to offer a diet drink using the brand name—was made for economic reasons. There simply wasn't enough money in the budget to properly advertise Diet Patio. Advertising Diet Pepsi along with Pepsi would generate enormous exposure for the new diet drink at a small price. Diet Pepsi was test-marketed in Detroit,

Michigan, and Louisville, Kentucky, and the results were measured by how many empties were returned to the bottling plants. Diet Pepsi proved to be a winner, and was then rolled out nationwide. Eventually, other soft drink manufacturers started using their brand names for their diet drinks.

Meanwhile, Pepsi-Cola had developed the Shopping Spree sweepstakes, which became a huge promotion in 1963 as well as in several subsequent years. Consumers who entered

*Pepsi's Shopping Spree promotion offered a chance for a family to gather all the groceries they could in a half an hour.*

*Pepsi took the unprecedented step of linking its brand name to a new diet drink in 1964.*

# Mountain Dew
## It'll tickle yore innards!

*In 1964, Pepsi bought Mountain Dew, a popular drink in the southeastern United States, and made it a national favorite.*

the Pepsi-sponsored contest could win a shopping spree at their local grocery store, whereby they could race through the aisles, grabbing everything they wanted off the shelves during an allotted time. The contest drew so much publicity that national magazines featured stories on the winners and their sprees. The contest and its sponsor became the subject of conversations at the water cooler and the dinner table as well as in shopping lines at the grocery store. The sweepstakes attracted 61 million entries.

One of the biggest success stories for Pepsi in 1964 was the acquisition of Mountain Dew. The Pepsi-Cola Company bought the soft drink from the Tip Corporation of Marion, Virginia, for a rumored $6 million in Pepsi-Cola stock. How the Tip Corporation, a company that marketed flavored drinks to bottlers, acquired the name and formula for the beverage is a matter of debate.

While one Bill Jones, a resident of Marion and the president of the Tip Corporation, is generally credited with concocting the Mountain Dew flavor that is familiar today, the Mountain Dew story actually begins elsewhere. Evidently, in the late 1940s, Hartman Beverage Company of Knoxville, Tennessee, bottled a lemon-lime drink they called Mountain Dew. Although this drink had some regional success, it never really caught on.

Fast forward to 1958, to beyond eastern Tennessee, where a respected soft drink supply salesman—Bill Jones—took over the Tip Corporation. In order to finance his new enterprise, Jones needed investors, so he offered shares in the new company to some

of his bottler friends. The original investors were Pepsi-Cola bottlers: Herman Minges of Lumberton, North Carolina; Richard Minges of Fayetteville, North Carolina; Allie Hartman of Knoxville, Tennessee; and Wythe Hull of Marion, Virginia.

142

At one of the first stockholders meetings of the new Tip Corporation, Hartman reportedly announced the donation, on behalf of his brother and him of their Mountain Dew drink to the new company. The addition of Mountain Dew to the product line would, it was hoped, give the company a competitive edge in the flavored drink market.

Rumor and speculation attend this transaction. One version has it that Jones was originally unwilling to accept the donation of the Mountain Dew name and formula, so Hartman proposed that Jones pay for their dinner, and they would call it even. If this story is true, one of the most valuable trademarks in the soft drink industry today was sold for a steak dinner—which reportedly cost $6.95.

Unfortunately for the Tip Corporation, at the same time that they were launching Mountain Dew, the Pepsi-Cola Company

*Because Mountain Dew had been developed by Pepsi-Cola bottlers, they had the first option on the franchise.*

was introducing its own lemon-lime drink, Teem. Most of Tip's customers were Pepsi bottlers who were reluctant to compete with the parent company, so they ended up selling Teem rather than Mountain Dew.

Meanwhile, an orange-based beverage called Golden Girl Cola, later named Sun Drop, was gaining popularity in a few of the Pepsi-Cola bottling territories operated by Tip investors. Jones was informed that Tip needed a drink to compete with Golden Girl.

Golden Girl had been developed by Charles Lazier of St. Louis, who was a friend of the Hartmans of Knoxville. Lazier claims to have originated the lemon-lime flavor that the Hartmans used for Mountain Dew—based on a drink Lazier created called Natural Set-Up. Golden Girl, or Sun Drop, thus evolved from a lemon-lime to an orange-based drink. The success of Sun Drop and competition from Teem consequently caused Jones to take Mountain Dew in a different direction, away from a lemon-lime flavor to an orangy taste.

Using Hull's Pepsi-Cola bottling facility as a base of operations, Jones began testing different formulas for Mountain Dew. Employees at the Marion Pepsi plant were the first to sample each new version of the drink. Finally, one mixture seemed to have the right taste.

This new Mountain Dew was test-marketed by the Mingeses with overwhelming success. Tip began to solicit Mountain Dew franchises; the company's shareholders agreed that Pepsi-Cola bottlers should be given the first opportunity at a charter. That's why most of the first Mountain Dew bottlers were also Pepsi-Cola bottlers.

Disney and Pepsi teamed up again in 1965 to produce one of the most popular attractions at the New York World's Fair.

Pepsi sponsored the exhibit, designed and constructed by Disney and called "It's a Small World—a Salute to UNICEF," the branch of the United Nations working to help children worldwide.

Exhibit patrons became passengers on a boat ride around the world, passing simulated Disney landscapes representing various countries and populated by dolls dressed in appropriate costumes. Heard in

various languages was the song "It's a Small World," composed by Dick and Bob Sherman. More than 3 million people visited the exhibit, which later became a featured attraction at Disneyland.

Over the years, a number of companies have approached Pepsi-Cola to negotiate a merger of one type or another. In the late 1950s, there had been serious talk about a merger with Pabst Brewing Co., makers of Pabst Blue Ribbon Beer, but it never materialized due to reservations by both boards. Then, in 1964, talks began regarding a merger with snack food company Frito-Lay of Dallas, Texas.

The subsequent merger resulted from the vision of the two principals, Herman Lay and Don Kendall, who believed that combining their two operations would create one of the world's most influential

# PEPSI POURS IT ON!

*The Pepsi-sponsored exhibit at the 1964–1965 New York World's Fair was created by Walt Disney. It was called "It's a Small World—a Salute to UNICEF."*

consumer products companies. The merger would in fact produce a company boasting a half-billion dollars in annual sales.

Frito-Lay was formed in 1961 with the merger of H.W. Lay and Company and the Frito Company. Frito began in 1932, when Elmer Doonlin bought the recipe and equipment to make a corn chip traditionally favored by the Mexican population of San Antonio, Texas. Doonlin paid $100 for the recipe and launched what would become one of the prominent foods in the snack business.

About the same time, hundreds of miles away in Nashville, Tennessee, Herman Lay began distributing potato chips for a company in Atlanta. Dissatisfied with the treatment he was getting from his supplier, Lay ended up buying the company, becoming both manufacturer and distributor. Frito became associated with Lay when he was granted a license to manufacture Fritos, an agreement that led to the merger of the two parties.

The merger between Pepsi-Cola and Frito-Lay was completed on January 10, 1965, with the signing of hundreds of papers that formed new companies and disbanded old ones. The resulting entity was called PepsiCo. Donald M. Kendall was named PepsiCo's president and chief executive officer, and Herman W. Lay became chairman of the board.

Pepsi and potato chips evidently went so well together that over the next 30 years, PepsiCo would become one of the most respected corporations in the world. Through the purchase of numerous fast food chains, PepsiCo has become a giant in the food service business. In 1996, PepsiCo sales topped $31 billion.

Given the size of PepsiCo, the decision was made to operate the divisions as separate companies, each with its own president. In October 1965, James B. Somerall assumed the presidency of Pepsi-Cola. Somerall, the first president of the company to have been a bottler, had been one of the many rising stars at Coca-Cola who followed Steele to Pepsi. After serving as president of Pepsi-Cola Cincinnati, he became vice president of Pepsi-Cola domestic operations before being named president of the company. One bottler said that Somerall "has forgotten more about the bottling business than most of us will ever learn."

The expansion of Pepsi-Cola and its new parent company, PepsiCo, continued through 1966. Overall sales had increased by 19 percent, pushing total revenue to more than $600 million. Meanwhile, to further expand its economic base, PepsiCo purchased North American Van Lines.

Over the previous 15 years, Pepsi-Cola had developed an efficient bottling and distribution system. Pepsi was available in a variety of sizes of bottles, including non-returnable bottles, and Pepsi in cans was gaining a share of the market.

In addition, sales and marketing of Diet Pepsi were moving along at a respectable pace. The song "Music to Watch Girls By," written exclusively for Diet Pepsi, was recorded by a number of popular recording artists, including trumpeter Al Hirt.

Teem and Patio were doing so well that Pepsi decided to offer another noncola beverage. This time the company entered the chocolate drink market with a product called Devil Shake—a name that was chosen after exhaustive consumer research eliminated 300 other contenders. Testing of the beverage yielded positive results, with one report even declaring it to be the best product of its kind. In one test market, New Haven, Missouri, Pepsi-Cola bottler Edward Hebbler said he was very pleased with the repeat purchases of Devil Shake.

The PEPSI GENERATION advertising theme was four years old in 1967, which meant it was time for a new campaign. To follow in the footsteps of such a successful campaign, however, posed a daunting challenge.

Eventually it was determined that ads would be created around the slogan TASTE THAT BEATS THE OTHERS COLD, PEPSI POURS IT ON!

**Summit meeting.**
Pepsi generation-style.

**All you need is a bright young point of view**
and a thirst for living.

**A thirst for Pepsi, too.**
Famous regular Pepsi-Cola
or new Diet Pepsi-Cola.

**Come on up.**
There's room at the top.

COME ALIVE! You're in the Pepsi generation!

Diverting from the image-building THINK YOUNG and COME ALIVE campaigns, PEPSI POURS IT ON promoted the taste of the product. This shift in emphasis was based on taste-testing research indicating that no other cola drink tasted as good as Pepsi, when properly chilled. Magazine ad copy declared *Drink Pepsi cold—the colder the better....that special Pepsi taste comes alive in the cold. Drenching, quenching taste that never gives out before your thirst gives in. Pepsi pours it on.*

*Diet Pepsi ads, aimed at women, emphasized the fact that the drink had only one calorie.*

*Diet Pepsi was originally advertised with Pepsi, but a separate advertising campaign was eventually created.*

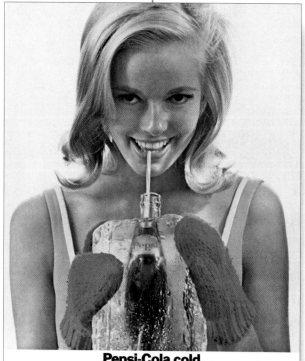

**Pepsi-Cola cold beats any cola cold!**

Drink Pepsi cold—the colder the better. Pepsi-Cola's taste was created for the cold. That special Pepsi taste comes alive in the cold. Drenching, quenching taste that never gives out before your thirst gives in. Pepsi pours it on!

Taste that beats the others cold... Pepsi pours it on!

**You've got a lot to live Pepsi's got a lot to give**

What we mean is this: living isn't always easy, but it never has to be dull. There's too much to see, to do, to enjoy. Put yourself behind a Pepsi-Cola and get started. You've got a lot to live.

*After the success of the* PEPSI GENERATION *campaign, Pepsi returned to product-related advertising.*

*Returning to the lifestyle advertising that had been so successful, Pepsi introduced the* YOU'VE GOT A LOT TO LIVE, PEPSI'S GOT A LOT TO GIVE *campaign in 1969.*

The creation of a jingle to go with the new advertising campaign was by now standard procedure. The new jingle, "Taste That Beats the Others Cold," performed by the vocal groups the Four Tops and the Hodells, was heard on radio and television commercials. This marked the beginning of the use of popular musicians to introduce Pepsi-Cola jingles.

While the COME ALIVE ad campaign had linked Pepsi and Diet Pepsi, the time had come for Diet Pepsi to step out on its own. Diet Pepsi's own advertising campaign was dubbed SOMEONE WILL BE WATCHING—it declared *The girls girl-watchers watch drink Diet Pepsi with only one calorie. Try it. Someone will be watching.*

Another diet drink produced by Pepsi was Tropic Surf. Researchers at Pepsi pushed for the introduction in 1968 of a low calorie, citrus-based drink, giving rise to a new slogan, BRACE YOURSELF FOR TROPIC SURF. In the next few years, however, Tropic Surf turned only modest profits.

In 1969, Pepsi launched another new advertising campaign, this one called YOU'VE GOT A LOT TO LIVE, PEPSI'S GOT A LOT TO GIVE. This slogan returned to the use of lifestyle themes.

The LIVE-GIVE theme may have been the most emotionally stimulating campaign created by Pepsi. Part of the motivation behind it was to offer an alternative to the cynical defensive stance toward life that young people were adopting in the late 1960s. The claim YOU'VE GOT A LOT TO LIVE promoted a life of openness, promise, and adventure. Ads proclaimed: *There's a new*

**148**

national pastime: living, and making every second count. Pepsi's part of it all, with the energy to let you live big, and a taste that's bigger than life. Pepsi-Cola—it's got a lot to give.

The LIVE-GIVE jingle, penned by Joe Brooks, was performed by the hottest musicians of the day, among them Johnny Cash, B.B. King, Three Dog Night, Tammy Wynette, and Friends of Distinction. The diversity of such artists increased Pepsi's appeal to all segments of the Pepsi Generation.

In all, the ad campaigns produced by Pepsi-Cola and BBDO in the 1960s were considered to be the best in the business. They broke new ground and set new standards. The key to their success was that they never forgot their audience.

The marketing people believed that the success of Pepsi-Cola advertising had been due to this simple formula: Take America's young people at play…add Pepsi and mix well. Commercials helped make Pepsi become the drink of young America in the '60s.

One of Pepsi's promotions during the 1960s involved the Women's Christian Temperance Union—a group opposed to the consumption of alcoholic beverages. Determined that U.S. troops in Vietnam have a soft drink on hand, the WCTU, in collaboration with Pepsi, distributed special store displays designed to collect funds to send the soft drink to soldiers serving in the war.

One of the most far-reaching innovations in the soft drink industry of the 1960s was convenience packaging, consisting of no-deposit no-return glass bottles and no-return metal flat-top cans. At first, the higher price for the nonreturnables slowed sales. Eventually, however, people chose to pay a little more for the convenience of not having to return bottles to the market. Consumers were also spending more time in their cars as well as in the outdoors—

both of which contributed to the growth of the new packaging.

The popularity of one-way bottles and cans was, however, exacerbating a growing problem in the United States—litter. This problem was a concern not only for Pepsi but for the entire soft drink industry. Pepsi responded by producing public service ads to raise awareness of the problem, and local Pepsi bottlers sponsored litter removal programs in their areas.

In 1969, Pepsi-Cola test-marketed a plastic Pepsi bottle for the first time. In the 1960s, plastic was being used in many new and different ways. There's a line in the 1967 hit movie, *The Graduate*: "The future is plastics." And Pepsi wanted its packaging ready for the future.

Indeed, Pepsi-Cola approached the end of the decade by preparing for the future. In 1965, the serrated cap logo was modified. In 1969, the graphics on Pepsi, Diet Pepsi, and Mountain Dew packaging got a new look, leading to a complete logo revision in the 1970s.

Sales for PepsiCo had reached nearly $1 billion by the close of 1969. It was hard to believe that just 20 years earlier, Pepsi-Cola had been on the verge of bankruptcy. The company's turnaround was nothing less than a financial miracle. No longer self-conscious about its past—about its struggles to secure financial stability and to present an image beyond that of a budget beverage—Pepsi-Cola looked forward to winning the cola wars of the 1970s.

*By the end of the 1960s, convenience became an important decision for consumers purchasing soft drinks.*

*The GOT A LOT TO GIVE campaign would lead the company into the 1970s.*

# have a pepsi day

Having accomplished considerable success in the previous two decades, Pepsi-Cola approached the 1970s with great anticipation. The challenges that lay ahead offered unparalleled opportunities for growth.

As evidence of the company's expansion, Pepsi-Cola had outgrown its headquarters at 500 Park Avenue. After nearly four decades in New York City, Pepsi-Cola relocated about an hour away in Purchase, New York. The new offices would be used by Pepsi-Cola and PepsiCo beginning in 1970.

At the time, the nation was experiencing a population explosion, as evidenced by the baby boomers (or "boomers"), who in the 1970s represented a formidable economic force. Moreover, boomers consumed the majority of available soft drinks—exceeding more than 200 cans per capita per year.

To reach this market, Pepsi had to stretch their creative muscles. While consumers in the '70s listed convenience, image, choice, and value as priorities, image was rated most highly among boomers. They demanded products that reflected the perceived spirit of their generation.

In 1970, the advertising campaign YOU'VE GOT A LOT TO LIVE, PEPSI'S GOT A LOT TO GIVE, begun in 1969, was still proving effective. Once again, Pepsi had hit a home run. The public's enthusiasm for this campaign was demonstrated by the thousands of letters Pepsi received expressing delight with its signature commercials and especially the theme song. Clearly, the tradition born with the original Pepsi-Cola jingle was still going strong.

One letter, from a San Francisco university official, offers the following praise:

*New graphics made Pepsi packaging more eye-catching in the supermarket.*

*The world came a step closer to peace in 1972, when an agreement was signed to sell Pepsi-Cola in the Soviet Union.*

JAN 6 1992    D. Fraser.

Holiday, 1981

Vol. 12, No. 5

## PEPSICO INK

### A Holiday Message

As the Holiday Season comes around again, we at PepsiCo can be thankful for many things, not least among them being another year of record growth for our company. We can all take pride in the fact that, in a difficult business environment, our revenues this year will exceed $7 billion — double that of just four years ago.

This achievement is the direct result of the dedication, imagination, and commitment which continues to be the trademark of PepsiCo people. It also shows what progress can be made by our teamwork in the face of today's economic climate. Each of you is to be congratulated for your important role in promoting our company to its present position of leadership in all of our divisions.

I extend warm holiday greetings to all and, as we turn the corner into 1982 together, another year of health, happiness and success to you and your family.

*Donald M. Kendall*

Headquarters in winter garb.

In this issue . . .

- Free tax booklet offered
  page 2
- Why Have a Fitness Profile?
  page 5
- Wilson's First Family of Running
  page 10

- PFI's Success Story
  page 12
- PepsiCo Challenger to puzzle you
  page 10
- A Liquid Love Story
  page 6

**IN RECOGNITION OF YOUR GENEROSITY**

The PepsiCo United Way Campaign for 1981 has reached an all-time high for the 11 years we have been in Westchester. Employee contributions have increased 23 percent over last year.

In this season of giving, it is good to know that you are sharing with others less fortunate.

---

*In 1970, Pepsi-Cola headquarters relocated to Purchase, New York, and shared space with the parent corporation, PepsiCo.*

*The upright cooler, known as a visi-cooler, indicated that Pepsi-Cola now offered a complete line of flavors and packaging.*

*This letter is to commend you on your new Pepsi-Cola commercials. Not only is the photography excellent and interesting, but the subject matter is timely and of high relevancy to today's youth. For once, real people enjoying today's real pleasures and entertainments are used in the advertising medium.... And the music is exciting, with the type of melody that stays with you. My whole office hums the tune all day.... Just tremendous. I hope that other companies will follow your excellence in making commercials for those of us who enjoy seeing TV commercials that are enjoyable.*

Another letter, from a Washington brewery executive, enthuses:

*The purpose of this letter is to tell you how very much I admire your new advertising campaign. I would very much like to obtain a recording of the sound tracks that accompany your TV commercials. My sole purpose in making this request is enjoyment of that fantastic music. If you have not made a record album for sale to the public I think you should consider the idea. If you already have, I am delighted and willing and ready to pay the normal costs. Congratulations on a great piece of business.*

In 1971, the company did in fact issue a recording that featured a selection of Pepsi jingles.

As conveyed in such letters, consumers embraced Pepsi ads during this era. The commercials garnered for Pepsi a positive feeling among the public for the product as well as for the company—they conveyed a

sense that Pepsi understood and appreciated the people who bought their soft drinks. Pepsi had grasped the notion that products sell primarily because of the way in which they reflect people's image of themselves and their lifestyle.

In the 1930s, Pepsi-Cola had been offered only in 12-ounce returnable bottles. By the 1970s, Pepsi was available in eight different sizes of returnable and nonreturnable containers. Pepsi also offered a variety of flavored soft drinks. Excluding fountain sales, most people bought soft drinks at supermarkets and convenience stores. The more sizes and styles of packaging that a company offered, the better equipped that company was to claim victory in the cola wars.

To compete in the complicated and combative market of the '70s, Pepsi-Cola sought a new president with a diversified background. Taking the helm of Pepsi-Cola in 1970, Vic Bonomo was the company's first president since Walter Mack who lacked experience in the soft drink industry. The thinking behind Bonomo's selection was that his tenure with the conglomerate General Foods had prepared him to pilot the growing Pepsi-Cola Company.

In Bonomo's first address to bottlers in September 1970, he began, as had many of his predecessors, by stating his belief in Pepsi-Cola's potential to be number one. He went on to explain how this could be achieved: by becoming a more modern professional company. He declared: "Intuition and gut reactions are still valuable and necessary, but they are no longer enough to run a successful business. Today's professional also needs great quantities of information and training in how to use it, in order to make valid decisions."

A quiet moment alone.
A chance to sort out yesterday's memories...
and put tomorrow in focus.
A chance to stretch out with a good book...
a warm sun...and an ice-cold Pepsi-Cola.
Pepsi has a taste as big as your tomorrow.
With energy to match.

**You've got a lot to live. Pepsi's got a lot to give.**

In other words, Pepsi would be guided by marketing data that had been analyzed by people trained in translating the data into increased sales. A.C. Nielsen, known for its television rating system, tabulated the consumption by brand of products for subscribing companies such as Pepsi. The numbers supplied by Nielsen were critical to the marketing people, as even a single point change in consumer brand preference signaled an increase or decrease of sales worth millions of dollars.

For almost 40 years, the Pepsi-Cola Company had been on an economic roller coaster, trying to survive. But following the company's unprecedented growth in the

*The LIVE-GIVE advertising campaign continued generating sales for Pepsi into the early 1970s.*

*This new logo, adopted in 1971, was part of an effort to give Pepsi a more modern and consistent appearance.*

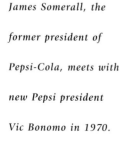

*James Somerall, the former president of Pepsi-Cola, meets with new Pepsi president Vic Bonomo in 1970.*

1960s, Pepsi-Cola shifted focus to devising ways to continue the fast-paced growth. If Pepsi aimed to be number one in the 1970s, it couldn't afford to take growth for granted. Pepsi needed to challenge the competition every day.

Thanks to effective national advertising, the image of Pepsi-Cola had improved over the years. Now it was time to establish a uniform logo on all products and equipment—by 1970, it had been anything goes, with old, new, and everything in-between appearing on various Pepsi products.

The consequent harm to the name recognition sought by Pepsi—not to mention the resulting decrease in sales—was alarming, especially as pointed out by the marketing people. They presented studies demonstrating the importance of logo identification in consumer purchasing, which meant that with hundreds of products sold in supermarkets, it was vital that consumers could readily identify products by their logo. Pepsi responded by launching a program called One Sight, One Sell.

This new program, aptly tied to the introduction of a new Pepsi logo in 1971, was spearheaded by Frank Rupp, Pepsi's vice president of graphic arts. Rupp had been a designer with the company's ad agency, BBDO, before being enticed to join the management at Pepsi. The One Sight, One Sell program was a joint production of Rupp's design team and the marketing department.

The goal of the nationwide effort was that every bottle, every sign, every truck, every ad—every anything—of Pepsi's appear with a uniform logo. Between 1971 and 1973—for the first time in company history—their products began to have a uniform look from community to community. One Sight, One Sell succeeded in increasing consumer awareness of Pepsi—and in increasing sales. In fact, Pepsi-Cola International adopted a similar program to yield comparable results overseas.

On the international front, Pepsi-Cola was making news by becoming the first American consumer product to be sold in the USSR. As early as 1959, when Pepsi had been featured at the Soviet Union Trade Exposition, Don Kendall hoped to someday open a bottling plant in that nation.

In the early 1970s, the Cold War between the United States and the Soviet Union was beginning to thaw. So when Kendall led a trade mission to the USSR in 1972, he gauged that the time was right to sell Pepsi to the Soviets. Signed that same year was an agreement between PepsiCo and the Soviet Foreign Trade Ministry that gave PepsiCo the right to bottle Pepsi in the Soviet Union. Technicians were promptly sent to the USSR to convert a beverage plant to a Pepsi-Cola bottling plant. By the end of 1973, Pepsi-Cola was being bottled and sold to the Soviet people, thanks to Don Kendall—and his good friend, President Richard Nixon.

## We found the smilin' majority were Pepsi people

Pounding on doors. Pinning on buttons. East, west, north and south, we worked at getting people interested. Getting them out to vote. And when our faces got as long as our days, ice-cold Pepsi-Cola made short work of it. Maybe the happy taste of Pepsi doesn't get everyone's vote...but it sure is a winner with the Smilin' Majority.

Clothes by Lady Wrangler and Mr. Wrangler divisions of Blue Bell Inc.  "PEPSI-COLA" AND "PEPSI" ARE REGISTERED TRADEMARKS OF PepsiCo, INC.

August, 1972, Glamour

*Although most of the company's advertising budget was funneled into television ads, magazines were still considered a valuable medium for advertising in the 1970s.*

*Using the same logo on all equipment and packaging was a way for Pepsi to maintain a positive image with the public.*

*Pepsi president Donald Kendall presents a gift to General Secretary Leonid Brezhnev upon Pepsi-Cola's introduction in the Soviet Union.*

By 1972, Pepsi-Cola was available in more than 125 countries around the world. Global expansion brought new challenges to Pepsi. Many countries in which Pepsi was sold lacked the hard currency to pay for the concentrate; Pepsi accepted payment in the form of goods. As a result, PepsiCo found itself bartering concentrate for locally produced goods the world over.

A notable example of how this bartering operated involved the Soviet Union, where, at the insistence of the Soviets, Pepsi was traded for vodka. This deal was a bit more complicated than most, particularly since an American company, Monsieur Henri Wines, held the rights to sales of Stolichnaya vodka in the United States. PepsiCo's solution was to purchase Monsieur Henri Wines for $26 million of PepsiCo stock. This deal resulted in PepsiCo becoming the exclusive U.S. distributor of Stolichnaya vodka.

In 1973, Pepsi-Cola marked its 75th anniversary, paying tribute to those who had contributed in helping the company come so far. Over the years of hardship and struggle, it had become clear that Pepsi-Cola's true asset was the people associated with the company—primarily the bottlers.

*In 1973, Pepsi introduced a new advertising campaign,* JOIN THE PEPSI PEOPLE FEELIN' FREE. *This campaign was in step with the* PEPSI GENERATION *advertising.*

Original Pepsi Girl

NEW
189
Birthp

NAEG

*Any celebration of the invention of Pepsi-Cola has always included a tip of the glass to New Bern, North Carolina, the product's birthplace.*

The highlight of the anniversary was a celebration in New Bern, North Carolina, the birthplace of Pepsi-Cola. A parade and other festivities commemorated Caleb Bradham's invention. Among the dignitaries in attendance were members of Bradham's family.

Pepsi's other big event of 1973 was a new advertising campaign, with a new song and a new slogan, JOIN THE PEPSI PEOPLE FEELIN' FREE. Ten years after introducing the concept of a Pepsi Generation, the company's advertising expanded to the Pepsi People. Who were the Pepsi People? Those who thought of themselves as individuals, who were open and independent, comfortable with being themselves and "feelin' free." Ads suggested that the taste of Pepsi complemented Americans' most dearly held notion—that of freedom. As in past campaigns, the aim was to appeal visually as well as emotionally.

In the early 1970s, Pepsi market researchers discovered that consumers tended to drink whatever amount of Pepsi they had at home—be it a single can or an entire case, if it was at home, people drank it. Therefore, if Pepsi wanted to increase sales, they needed to persuade the public to bring more Pepsi into their homes.

To encourage such behavior, Pepsi began to offer its products in packaging that was considered consumer-friendly. Pepsi's introduction in 1972 of the 12-pack derived from the company's intention to boost sales in the take-home market.

One year later, Pepsi introduced the 64-ounce bottle, which offered consumers considerable convenience and value. Marketed as The Boss because of its size, the big bottle had a less flattering name among Pepsi drivers, as a case of eight such bottles was quite hefty. Eventually, to the relief of many, the heavy glass bottles would be replaced by lighter plastic ones.

*In 1973, Pepsi-Cola introduced a 64-ounce returnable bottle called The Boss.*

**160**

The power of the Challenge expands the soft drink category growth in your store

Here's what we mean:

**Category Growth**

| Markets | 12 Months Before Challenge | 12 Months With Challenge |
|---|---|---|
| Boston | + 5% | + 9% |
| Jacksonville | + 12% | + 28% |
| Nashville | + 10% | + 20% |
| Los Angeles | + 1% | + 5% |
| Minneapolis | + 7% | + 13% |

Translate these percentages into additional case sales and you can realize the momentum the Challenge generates for the soft drink category.

Since we introduced the Pepsi Challenge in the category has grown in our market at the following rate:

| 12 MONTHS BEFORE CHALLENGE | 12 MONTHS WITH CHALLENGE |
|---|---|
| | |

At the Pepsi-Cola Bottlers Convention in 1973, speeches by Pepsi executives repeated the refrain heard in years past: "We can be number one.... We can beat Coke."

Suddenly, that goal was close at hand. The gap between Coke and Pepsi was narrowing. In his address to the bottlers, Kendall proclaimed, "I think next year if we all work together, we can advance one more notch toward that goal. Because we're Pepsi People, and we're destined to be number one!"

In 1974, Pepsi-Cola pulled even with Coca-Cola in food store sales. To Pepsi, this was the critical front in the cola wars—the one place where consumer preference could be accurately measured.

The soft drink industry is made up of three markets: fountain, vending, and retail outlets. Fountain and vending are captive markets. The consumer doesn't have much of a choice—he or she only has

the option of the cola drink offered by the establishment providing the fountain service or vending machine. But in supermarkets and other food stores, the consumer can choose from the array of colas appearing on the shelves.

By 1977, Pepsi-Cola actually pulled ahead of Coke in the arena of consumer preference. After years of battling to stay alive, Pepsi had won a big victory, ranking number one in the food store segment of the market. Although Coke disputed this finding, the fallen giant offered no evidence to the contrary. The Nielsen numbers spoke for themselves—Pepsi was number one in this market.

While Pepsi had been closing the gap with Coke for years, arguably it was the PEPSI GENERATION ads and packaging that enabled Pepsi to move into the lead—clinched by one of the most effective advertising programs ever launched: TAKE THE PEPSI CHALLENGE.

*In the 1970s, the supermarket became the major battlefield between Pepsi and Coke.*

*The Pepsi Challenge let consumers make up their own minds about which cola taste they preferred.*

*Once the Pepsi Challenge*

*succeeded regionally,*

*it was introduced*

*nationwide.*

In the years since 1934 and the introduction of the 12-ounce bottle for a nickel, Pepsi-Cola had penetrated every market in the country except that existing below the Mason-Dixon line. This line, which traditionally separates the United States into North and South, also separated Coca-Cola drinkers from Pepsi drinkers. With the exception of the Carolinas, the South was Coke country.

In Dallas, Texas, Pepsi ran a distant third behind Coke and Dr. Pepper. Pepsi's national advertising didn't seem to have much influence on the habitual cola drinkers of that city. The Dallas Pepsi manager hired a local ad agency to investigate.

The results upset commonly held assumptions. Surveys conducted by the agency revealed that Coke drinkers preferred Coke because of its taste, not because of the Coca-Cola name or image. Furthermore, in taste testing conducted for research studies, most participants claimed to prefer the taste of Pepsi.

Armed with this knowledge, Pepsi strategists worked to determine how they could turn things in Dallas. They believed that keeping the measurable issue of taste at the forefront would prove more effective for Pepsi than fighting a battle over something as intangible as image.

Blind taste tests, in which samples are not identified, were pursued with subjects who had claimed not only to prefer the taste of Coke over Pepsi but also to be able to tell the two drinks apart by their taste. In fact, when unaware of which cola they were sampling, of the initial group of participants who claimed to prefer Coke, 50 percent said that Pepsi tasted better.

These results, demonstrating that Pepsi could beat Coke among die-hard Coca-Cola drinkers, quickly caught the public's attention. The test results also gave birth to what became known as the PEPSI CHALLENGE.

The theme of the ad campaign involved everyday people being filmed as they took up the challenge to choose Coke over Pepsi when unaware of which cola they were drinking. Many of the people featured in PEPSI CHALLENGE commercials became local celebrities—which only added to the campaign's success.

These commercials owed much of their popularity to their apparent spontaneity and unscripted quality. Most product comparison advertising at the time was viewed with skepticism because of its obvious bias toward the advertiser. In contrast, the use of real people discovering for themselves that they preferred the taste of Pepsi won these commercials high marks for credibility. To enhance their credibility, the commercials occasionally even showed a participant choosing Coke over Pepsi.

In addition to television commercials, the campaign consisted of live taste tests held throughout the country. The success of these events was borne out by the long lines of people eager to take the challenge. A majority of the participants did, in fact, end up preferring the taste of Pepsi. Their reactions ranged from disbelief to excitement—as if they had won some kind of contest by choosing Pepsi over Coke.

An added benefit of the live tests was that the local press seemed to think that they made good copy. Besides the free publicity, such press coverage contributed to the credibility of the campaign.

*The Pepsi Challenge became such a powerful marketing tool that it soon became part of all Pepsi advertising.*

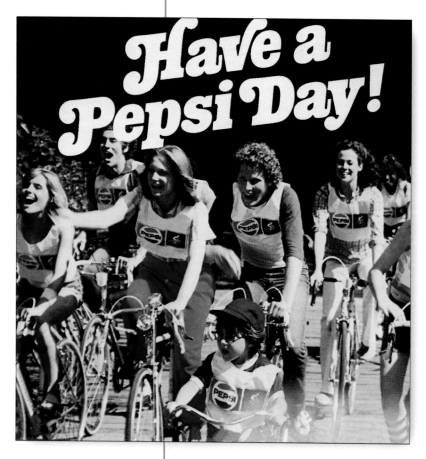

*The HAVE A PEPSI DAY campaign featured young people drinking Pepsi while experiencing the best that life has to offer.*

*The HAVE A PEPSI DAY slogan was appropriated from a then-popular phrase: "Have a nice day."*

Many would argue that the Pepsi Challenge was the most significant event in the history of the cola wars. They would also argue that the success of the program and its various incarnations was what led Coca-Cola to tinker with its formula for the first time.

Every one of Pepsi's past successes had been dismissed by Coca-Cola for one reason or another. And in each case, Coca-Cola was able to engage in one-upmanship to offset any gains Pepsi may have made. Pepsi's move to larger and more convenient packaging, for example, was only a temporary setback for Coca-Cola, as they could offer the same. But when it came to the Pepsi Challenge, Coca-Cola was powerless. People either liked the taste of the soft drink, or they didn't—and, according to surveys, more often people preferred the taste of Pepsi.

At first, Coca-Cola ridiculed the challenge results. When that backfired, the company tried to out-advertise Pepsi. When that failed, Coca-Cola resorted to slashing prices in an area where a challenge was taking place, in an attempt to derail the event.

All the evidence suggests that the Pepsi Challenge was engendering self-doubt within the Coca-Cola Company. Until that skirmish, Coca-Cola had been confident of its victory in the cola wars—simply because Coke was "The Real Thing," and anything else was an imitation. Now that taste comparisons had leveled the playing field, Coca-Cola discovered that its name alone was no longer sufficient to conquer competitors.

In 1908, Pepsi-Cola had persuaded auto racer Barney Oldfield to endorse its product, starting a trend of securing the services of celebrities to sell Pepsi. Most simply appeared in the ads, drinking Pepsi. In 1975, Pepsi took celebrity endorsements to another level with Brazilian soccer star Pelé, whose fans spanned the globe. In the United States—one of the few nations of the world where soccer is not the most popular sport—Pepsi invested money in youth soccer programs that Pelé himself had developed.

In 1976, the FEELIN' FREE ad campaign was replaced with HAVE A PEPSI DAY! As America was celebrating its bicentennial, Pepsi was staying in touch with the Pepsi Generation. This new theme co-opted a greeting then endemic—"Have a nice day." Pepsi again reached consumers by speaking to their time as well as to their most optimistic view of themselves and their world.

The PEPSI DAY campaign featured some of the finest Pepsi Generation commercials. One, titled "Pony," featured a father and son on their ranch. As the father opens the barn to reveal a pony, the boy's face lights up with joy. It's not the pony, however, that delights him so (horses have always been around the ranch)—it's a new bicycle.

In 1976, Pepsi-Cola launched a new weapon in the cola wars: a soft drink dubbed Pepsi Light. This low-calorie cola contained a hint of lemon flavoring. Initial response was favorable, but sales eventually dropped too low for the company to continue manufacturing the beverage. A small but loyal group of Pepsi Light drinkers hopes to this day that their favorite drink will someday return.

John Sculley became president of Pepsi-Cola in 1977, replacing Vic Bonomo, who had been promoted to a vice president of PepsiCo. At age 38, Sculley was the youngest president in the history of the Pepsi-Cola Company. After graduating from Brown University, Sculley had enrolled in the University of Pennsylvania to study architecture. But he found himself fascinated by marketing. Encouraged by his wife's stepfather—who happened to be Donald Kendall—Sculley switched to the university's school of business, where he eventually received his M.B.A.

Fresh out of business school, Sculley landed a job with an advertising firm. In time, he found himself working for Pepsi, where he distinguished himself in marketing. Ten years later, he was president and CEO of the company. Under Sculley's leadership, Pepsi continued its tremendous growth.

Since the beginning of Pepsi-Cola's resurgence in the 1930s, management felt it necessary to own bottling plants. Pepsi eventually acquired 20 plants, with the exact number fluctuating from year to year. These company-owned plants were run as a separate entity called Pepsi-Cola Metropolitan Bottling Company, with most of the operations being in large cities.

As the original Pepsi-Cola bottlers from the 1930s began to retire or die, a large number of family-owned plants went up for sale. To make sure that they were

*In 1977, 38-year-old John Sculley became Pepsi-Cola's youngest president.*

**165**

*Pelé, the world-famous soccer star, became Pepsi's first international superstar endorser.*

run properly, the parent company ended up buying many of them. In 1978, the coalition of company-owned plants was renamed the Pepsi-Cola Bottling Group—the world's largest bottling operation.

Added to Pepsi's product line in 1978 was Aspen, a low-calorie apple-flavored soft drink. The theme THE NEW SOFT DRINK WITH JUST A SNAP OF APPLE introduced the beverage to the public. Although Aspen did well in test markets, it never developed a strong following.

Meanwhile, in the late 1970s, Pepsi's 64-ounce glass bottle was replaced by a plastic 2-liter bottle. The growing availability of convenient, one-way packaging and its encouragement of a throwaway society continued to foster concern about damage to the natural world and its effect on the health and safety of the population. Many states responded by adopting deposit laws on nonreturnable packaging in an effort to force consumers to recycle.

Another national issue that directly involved Pepsi-Cola in the 1970s was a Federal Trade Commission (FTC) ruling that franchise territories were illegal. In other words, allowing only one bottler to sell Pepsi in a certain geographic area was determined to be bad for competition. This decision threatened the livelihood of hundreds of family-owned Pepsi bottlers as well as bottlers of other soft drinks.

Against the FTC's contention that franchise territories adversely affected competition, the nation's bottlers argued that competition was between brands, not between bottlers. This battle went on for more than nine years, with Pepsi bottlers at the forefront.

On July 9, 1980, President Jimmy Carter signed into law the Soft Drink Interbrand Competition Act, which protected the franchise bottler from antitrust suits in the future. If the law hadn't been passed, the value of a Pepsi-Cola franchise—many of which had been built into businesses worth millions—would have diminished to almost nothing.

As the decade drew to an end, Pepsi-Cola again launched a new advertising campaign. CATCH THAT PEPSI SPIRIT became Pepsi's battle cry in 1979. Using the model that had proved so effective, commercials and print ads depicted people enjoying life, Pepsi in hand. This new advertising campaign endured until 1981.

As Pepsi-Cola was expanding, so was PepsiCo. In 1977, the corporation acquired the Pizza Hut chain, which included more than 2,000 outlets across the United States. PepsiCo's ambition to enter the restaurant market wasn't satisfied by owning just one chain. The following year, the corporation purchased Taco Bell and emerged as a major player in the restaurant industry.

By the end of 1979, PepsiCo sales amounted to more than $5 billion, with more than $2 billion coming from soft drink sales. The advertising campaigns and promotions of the 1970s had yielded steady gains in sales and market share. Moreover, Pepsi ranked number one in the all-important food store market. Never before had Pepsi's future been so secure.

*Pepsi Light, a low calorie cola drink with a taste of lemon, was introduced in 1976.*

Catch that Pepsi Spirit!

*To further diversify, PepsiCo entered the highly competitive restaurant business by purchasing Pizza Hut in 1977.*

# the choice of
# a new generation

By 1980, the difficulties of Pepsi's past were a distant memory. Most Pepsi employees—as well as the public—saw Pepsi as one of the world's two leading cola companies, battling relentlessly to be considered number one.

With John Sculley, the whiz kid of soft drinks, in charge, along with his innovative marketing team, sales and market share continued to rise. It was only a matter of time before Pepsi would dominate the market.

In 1981, Pepsi's new advertising campaign proclaimed PEPSI'S GOT YOUR TASTE FOR LIFE! As in the past, ads appealed to a life of optimism and freedom. The results, however, were not as dynamic as those resulting from the PEPSI GENERATION campaigns, and the theme was dropped two years later.

Meanwhile, the PEPSI CHALLENGE promotion was still producing remarkable boosts in sales wherever the promotions were held. The public was more than willing to let their taste buds decide the victor in the cola wars. The challenge was undoubtedly Pepsi's prime weapon against Coke. The promotion would be reinforced in later years through catchphrases like TASTE THE WINNING TASTE and LET YOUR TASTE DECIDE.

Pepsi's advertising success in the 1960s and 1970s posed a dilemma for the marketing and advertising people of the 1980s. BBDO, Pepsi's ad agency, along with such Pepsi advertising people as Alan Pottasch, had made it look easy to produce great campaigns, and the public's expectations of advertising had grown considerably. As Pepsi's advertising team met to plan 1983's campaign, their task was a formidable one: to create a promotion that not only met the standards set by the past but also exceeded them.

*In the 1980s, commercials featuring musical superstars such as Michael Jackson, Madonna, and the legendary Ray Charles bolstered Pepsi's image for a new generation.*

*Pepsi's "Archeology" commercial won a Clio award for best technical commercial of 1985.*

Here's to 25 more great years!

Let your taste decide.
Take the Pepsi Challenge!

PEPSI

**Pepsi's proud to be served at the Happiest Place on Earth.**

Pepsi-Cola has been a refreshing hit at Disneyland ever since the park opened. Pepsi just seems to go naturally with excitement, laughter and old-fashioned fun.

We look forward to many more successful years of association with Disneyland — the Happiest Place on Earth.

Cheers!

PEPSI

Bottled by Pepsi-Cola Bottling Co. of Los Angeles under appointment from PepsiCo, Inc., Purchase, N.Y.

*In 1980, Pepsi saluted Disneyland on the park's 25th anniversary.*

Their first attempt, with the OH, WHAT A TIME FOR PEPSI slogan, was previewed for Pepsi executives in the fall of 1982. The reaction was far from enthusiastic. After a good deal of thinking, the campaign was changed to PEPSI NOW!

The PEPSI NOW! campaign debuted in early 1983 at the Pepsi bottlers convention. It deftly combined hard sell and "heart" sell, mixing the magic of the PEPSI GENERATION with the power and persuasiveness of the PEPSI CHALLENGE. And, of course, it featured a catchy jingle. As the lyric stated, "It's gonna be Pepsi now!" Laying down the gauntlet, Pepsi announced that the new campaign would be so successful that

Coke, which was using the slogan COKE IS IT, would have to change that slogan to COKE WAS IT.

Also celebrated at the convention was the 20th anniversary of the introduction of the PEPSI GENERATION ads. The hope was that PEPSI NOW! would mark the beginning of another 20 years of highly acclaimed, award-winning advertising.

The convention was also memorable for John Sculley's remarkable address to the bottlers. Instead of stressing marketing, which was his background, Sculley emphasized the increasing importance of computers to the businesses of the bottlers. Most attendees found his remarks odd, and some questioned his motives, primarily because, following the convention, Sculley resigned from Pepsi to become president and CEO of Apple Computers.

Sculley's resignation was a shock to the Pepsi organization, for he left just as the company was gearing up for the challenges of the new decade. Most disappointed was Don Kendall, who had been a friend and mentor to Sculley.

In a surprise move, Pepsi named Roger Enrico president of the company. Such changes in leadership are usually planned and executed with a minimum of interruption. Yet all of a sudden, Enrico found himself in charge of Pepsi-Cola, now called Pepsi USA.

After leaving General Mills in 1971 to work for Frito-Lay as an associate brand manager, Enrico had served in various positions throughout PepsiCo. In 1982, he became an executive vice president of Pepsi-Cola, serving as an advisor to Sculley.

Enrico took over Pepsi-Cola in the midst of the success of the PEPSI CHALLENGE. And Coca-Cola, incensed over both the publicity of people choosing Pepsi in taste test after taste test and Pepsi's resulting market share increase, was determined to fight back. Coca-Cola's first big move was to switch to a combination of sugar and corn syrup as a less expensive way of sweetening Coke, thus providing additional funds to boost the advertising budget.

Pepsi responded by examining the Pepsi formula, which was more delicately balanced than Coke's. When combined with Pepsi's other ingredients, the corn syrup produced in the early 1980s did not result in a savory drink. This prompted Enrico to pressure corn syrup producers to develop a sweetener that would preserve the challenge-winning taste of Pepsi. As long as Pepsi was paying for sugar as its sweetener, Coke could boast an estimated $120 million profit advantage.

Another problem faced by Enrico was the need to increase the price of Pepsi concentrate to the bottlers. Most of the parent company's profit came from selling the concentrate, but while raising the price would give the corporation more money, it would also force the bottler to raise his price, potentially shrinking his profits. The bottlers weren't prepared for this and, after working as president for only a few months, Enrico found himself in the midst of a confrontation. In a meeting with the bottlers' representative, Enrico pleaded his case for a price increase. The bottlers wouldn't back down. Eventually, Enrico compromised, delaying the price increase for six months. By that time, the corn sweetener would be ready, thus offsetting the price increase. The bottlers were satisfied and heartened that Enrico was willing to work with them.

Pepsi needed to introduce some big promotion. Several recent ads had caught the imagination and interest of the public, but most had been simply good advertising.

"PEPSI," "PEPSI-COLA," AND "PEPSI'S GOT YOUR TASTE FOR LIFE" ARE REGISTERED TRADEMARKS OF PEPSICO, INC.

So Andrall Pearson, president of PepsiCo, called on Enrico shortly after he was named president of Pepsi-Cola USA, and suggested that Pepsi needed some big ideas to get things going. Enrico came up with a blockbuster of an idea. He decided to revitalize Pepsi advertising through a program that would recapture the magic of the original PEPSI GENERATION campaign.

The first step in creating the new PEPSI GENERATION advertising was to persuade Alan Pottasch not to retire. Considered by many to be the father of the Pepsi Generation, the loss of Pottasch would

*The slogan* PEPSI'S GOT YOUR TASTE FOR LIFE! *was used from 1981 until 1983. The imagery was very much like that used in previous* PEPSI GENERATION *campaigns.*

*Trying to find a campaign as innovative as the*
PEPSI GENERATION, *Pepsi introduced the*
PEPSI NOW! *slogan in 1983.*

*Pepsi promoted the Pepsi Challenge by*
*sponsoring racing competitors like Don*
*"Snake" Prudhomme.*

*Company president Roger Enrico began the trend of using superstars such as Tina Turner in Pepsi commercials.*

make it difficult to put together new advertising. To lure him back, Enrico suggested that they recreate the PEPSI GENERATION advertising campaign. Pottasch agreed to postpone his retirement.

In concert with the people at BBDO, Pottasch developed some of the most imaginative commercials in Pepsi's history. The slogan for the new ad campaign was PEPSI–THE CHOICE OF A NEW GENERATION. Satisfied with the commercial but not dazzled by the slogan, Enrico told the advertising people to come up with something better.

The big event that would launch the NEW GENERATION campaign appeared out of the blue. The Jacksons, featuring Michael Jackson, arguably the most important entertainer of the 1980s, were preparing a 1984 reunion tour. When Pepsi was offered the chance to sponsor the tour, Enrico thought it was a good idea, but he didn't know just how good it would turn out for Pepsi.

After viewing some of Michael Jackson's videos, Enrico inquired about the price for sponsoring the tour. He was quoted the astronomical figure of $5 million. Once over the shock, and ready to negotiate, Enrico was told that he now needed to deal with boxing promoter Don King, who was promoting the tour.

Enrico's quick acceptance of such an outrageously high price for the sponsorship may have been a preemptive strike against the possibility that Coke would sponsor Jackson. After days of negotiations, the contracts were signed on November 11, 1983, and Pepsi became the official sponsor of the Jacksons' 1984 Victory Tour. Pepsi had

paid for the privilege of making two commercials featuring the Jacksons, and holding press conferences in which the Jacksons would appear.

In a hastily called press conference, Enrico proclaimed that Pepsi and the Jacksons were going to make magic together. In the months to come, Michael Jackson, BBDO, and Pepsi would produce one of the greatest commercials in the history of advertising. At the press conference, Jackson whispered to Enrico, "Roger, I'm going to make Coke wish they were Pepsi."

After the exhilaration of the press conference had subsided, Pepsi's sponsorship was barely mentioned in news reports about the Jacksons' Victory Tour.

*Pepsi ad man Alan Pottasch worked day and night to make the Michael Jackson commercial a success.*

*In 1984, Michael Jackson became the highest paid celebrity endorser in the history of the Pepsi-Cola Company.*

*The Jacksons' 1984*

*Victory Tour promoted*

*Pepsi sales wherever the*

*group performed.*

Background: The great challenge for Roger Enrico was to continue Pepsi's phenomenal growth while leading the company into the 1980s.

To recreate the excitement of the original PEPSI GENERATION advertising campaign, Pepsi introduced THE CHOICE OF A NEW GENERATION in 1984.

Signing Michael Jackson to do a Pepsi commercial was just the kind of publicity needed to launch the NEW GENERATION campaign.

It didn't matter whether it was Michael Jackson or the Pepsi Challenge that caused Coke to change. It was obvious to all that Coke was trying to taste like The Choice of a New Generation.

With $5 million on the line, Pepsi had to do something to get more publicity for the investment, so the company decided to announce publicly that Pepsi was paying the Jacksons the greatest amount of money ever paid for a television commercial. Instantly, phone calls and letters requesting interviews and information about the commercials flooded Pepsi's offices. Finally Pepsi had a big event with which to launch the PEPSI—CHOICE OF A NEW GENERATION campaign.

In the end, it proved more difficult to actually make Pepsi commercials featuring the Jacksons than it did to have them sign the contracts. The biggest problems arose when some of Michael Jackson's celebrity friends raised concerns that he was overexposing himself, and he decided that he was not happy with the agreement made with Pepsi. To try to resolve this problem, Alan Pottasch from Pepsi and Phil Dusenberry from BBDO flew to Los Angeles to meet with Jackson. With storyboards in hand, they showed Jackson what they had in mind for the commercial. Jackson didn't like the lyrics or the song that BBDO had written to go with the commercials. He especially was unhappy about how often his face appeared. The overexposure issue was central to all of Jackson's concerns.

It was obvious that Jackson didn't want to do the commercials. All calls were referred to his lawyer, who said that the problems could be solved by payment of another $5 million. Enrico was unwilling to stray from the original contract. Finally, Pottasch reached Jackson's parents, who arranged a meeting with Pepsi. In the meeting, Jackson said that it wasn't that he didn't want to make the commercials, he just wanted to make them differently, and he suggested a number of changes that were acceptable to the advertising team. He wanted to replace the BBDO song with a rewritten version of his hit "Billie Jean." Pepsi was astounded by this turn of events—Jackson had offered his hit song, along with a number of creative changes, in exchange for fewer close-ups.

The team immediately began shooting the commercials. As the finishing touches were put on the final commercial, the fireworks used during the shoot set Jackson's hair on fire. He was rushed to the hospital, but wasn't severely hurt. The question of liability was settled after Pepsi made a generous donation to the burn center where Jackson had been treated.

When the commercials were finally ready for airing, Jackson was again unhappy. He felt that Pepsi had reneged on its agreement to limit his face time, and after several discussions, Pepsi edited the commercials to Jackson's liking. The final edits were done just hours before the debut of the commercials during the 1984 Grammy Awards.

*"Chase," a 4½-minute cliffhanger commercial featuring Michael Jackson, debuted in 1987.*

179

Reprinted by permission, Tribune Media Services

TASTING IN PROGRESS

Coca-Cola

"EUREKA, GENTLEMEN! WE'VE GOT IT! IT TASTES JUST LIKE PEPSI!!"

*Because of declining sales, Coca-Cola reformulated its 100-year-old secret formula in 1985.*

It may have been the most anticipated commercial in television history. MTV offered to show the commercial for free just to be able to show it first, and even planned a one-hour special focusing on the Jackson commercials.

Fortunately for Pepsi, the media couldn't get enough of the Michael Jackson commercial hype. The public relations department at Pepsi worked overtime to fulfill all of the requests for interviews with company executives. Jackson lived up to his promise, and Pepsi received an enormous amount of publicity.

The 1984 advertisements won numerous awards and received high consumer ratings. They were said to be some of the best commercials ever made for television. But they were a tough act to follow, and Pepsi needed to come up with an equally spectacular campaign for 1985.

BBDO did just that, creating better commercials for the 1985 campaign. The "Archeology" commercial was judged the best commercial in the world for 1985. In the futuristic commercial, a professor is leading his archeology class on a dig where they discover an oddly shaped bottle. One of the students asks what it is, and the professor replies, "I don't know!" The relic is an old Coke bottle.

During the hectic period prior to making the Michael Jackson commercial, Pepsi had considered signing pop star Lionel Ritchie. Impressed with Ritchie's work, Enrico offered him a contract to work for Pepsi in 1985. As a follow-up to the Jackson commercial, Pepsi made two commercials with Ritchie and sponsored his 1985 world tour. "Block Party" became one of the biggest—and most expensive—commercials Pepsi had ever made.

But the big commercial story of 1985 wasn't in advertising. It was the introduction of New Coke.

One year before Coca-Cola's 100th anniversary, they decided to change their cola formula. All kinds of folklore still circulate about the Coca-Cola formula—the president of the company is the only one who has it; it is kept in a safe-deposit box and only the president of the company can retrieve it; all of the ingredients used to make Coca-Cola are labeled with a number so that no one actually knows what is used in making the syrup.

In April 1985, Coca-Cola called a press conference to announce the soft drink's reformulation. When asked why they changed the formula, the company replied that while experimenting with Diet Coke, they had created a new and better taste for Coke, and consumer tests had shown that people liked this new Coke better than the traditional one.

Pepsi believed that 30 years of Coca-Cola losing market shares to Pepsi forced the company to make the change. New Coke in fact tasted much like Pepsi, which led Pepsi to believe that Coke had finally figured out Pepsi's secret to success—Pepsi actually tasted better than Coke.

The timing of the introduction of New Coke seemed to correspond with the death of Robert Woodruff, the former president and longtime patriarch of the Coca-Cola Company. Many believed that as long as Woodruff was alive, he would not allow any changes to the formula. Pepsi decided to take full advantage of the situation by announcing that Pepsi had just won the cola war. Pepsi believed that Coca-Cola had changed the long-time formula because it could no longer compete against the taste of Pepsi. Most industry observers agreed that New Coke was an attempt to make Coca-Cola taste like Pepsi. But what Coca-Cola ended up with was a cola that didn't taste as good

A SPECIAL EDITORIAL CARTOON ISSUE OF PepsiWorld

*Changing the Coca-Cola formula was a pivotal moment in the cola wars. By doing so, Coke admitted that Pepsi tasted better.*

**PEPSI. THE CHOICE OF A NEW GENERATION.™**

In 1985, pop star Lionel Ritchie carried the NEW GENERATION promotion into its second year.

*Lionel Richie*

as Pepsi and tasted worse than the original Coke. This change was a dire miscalculation and a huge blunder for Coca-Cola. Public demand eventually forced Coca-Cola to bring back the original formula.

Not willing to let Coca-Cola's mistake go unnoticed, Pepsi took out a full-page ad in the *New York Times* and other major newspapers to announce that Pepsi had won the cola war. The advertisement appeared as a letter addressed to Pepsi bottlers and Pepsi-Cola Company personnel. It read: "After 87 years of going eyeball to eyeball, the other guy just blinked. Coke is withdrawing their product from the marketplace and is reformulating Coke to be more like Pepsi." The letter also announced that Pepsi employees were being given a day off to celebrate the victory.

Pepsi aired television commercials that focused on how it might have felt for Coke drinkers to have their beloved cola taken away with no explanation. At the end of the commercial, the Coke drinkers take a sip of Pepsi and reply, "Now I know why." The commercials were a tremendous success, which precipitated a rise in Pepsi sales.

By July 1985, Coca-Cola decided to bring back the original Coke as Classic Coke. For a year, Coca-Cola actually sold two Coke products: New Coke and Classic Coke. But Coca-Cola withdrew New Coke from the market in April 1986. Coke's disastrous year was ridiculed in cartoon strips and mocked by comedians in 1985 and 1986. Pepsi employees reveled in the knowledge that they had beaten Coke. Hard work, a popular product, clever advertising,

*Film and television star Michael J. Fox starred in some of Pepsi's most popular television commercials of the 1980s.*

**183**

*While Coke was being reformulated, Pepsi continued producing such award-winning commercials as "Sound Truck."*

184

We've got the 100% Solution. 100% NutraSweet.

*In 1984 Pepsi became the first major soft drink to contain 100 percent NutraSweet.*

*Slice, a brand of flavored drinks containing 10 percent fruit juice, was introduced by Pepsi in 1984.*

and the Pepsi Challenge itself had toppled the giant from Atlanta.

Pepsi's 1986 CHOICE OF A NEW GENERATION commercial featured many stars. Don Johnson, from the hit television show "Miami Vice," and Glenn Frey of the Eagles were featured in a commercial entitled "Dance." Michael J. Fox was featured in his first Pepsi commercial, called "The Power of Suggestion." When asked why he decided to do a commercial for Pepsi, Fox said, "because Pepsi is creative and classy." Billy Crystal appeared in a commercial for Diet

Pepsi. Pepsi signed Michael Jackson to another contract in 1986.

In 1986, after nearly 40 years with Pepsi-Cola and PepsiCo, Don Kendall stepped down as chairman of the board. D. Wayne Calloway, who had spent most of his PepsiCo career at Frito-Lay, became the new chairman of the board. In 1987, Roger Enrico was promoted to president of PepsiCo World Wide Beverages. Craig Weatherup, president of Pepsi Bottling Group, was made president of Pepsi-Cola.

The sensational advertising program of the 1980s overshadowed some of the other things that had happened at Pepsi. Between 1980 and 1989, soft drink sales had risen from $2 billion to almost $6 billion. In 1983, Burger King became Pepsi's largest national account. Finally, after several years of effort, Pepsi unseated Coke as the industry leader.

Diet Pepsi-Cola, introduced in 1964, had been embattled for years by public interest groups protesting the use of artificial sweeteners. At first, the soft drink industry was banned from using artificial sweeteners containing cyclamates. Then, in the 1970s, attempts were made to ban saccharin. Some soft drink companies blended the new better-tasting aspartame (NutraSweet) with saccharin, but in 1984, Diet Pepsi became the first soft drink in the world to sell a diet cola made with 100 percent aspartame.

To keep the company growing, Pepsi began adding new products in the 1980s. Pepsi responded to consumer demand for caffeine-free drinks by introducing Pepsi Free and Diet Pepsi Free in 1983. In 1984, Pepsi introduced a lemon-lime soda containing 10 percent fruit juice, called Slice. Later, the company introduced orange, apple, and cherry-cola Slice. By 1986, Slice sodas generated $1 billion in annual sales.

In 1987, Pepsi sponsored the United States' entry in the America's Cup Sailboat Race. Critics viewed Dennis Conner, the captain of *The Stars and Stripes*, as an underdog in the international competition. But, just as the small, almost thrice bankrupt Pepsi Company had overcome innumerable odds to beat Coca-Cola in the cola wars, *The Stars and Stripes* won the America's Cup. As the sailboat crossed the finish line, the enormous sail featuring the Pepsi logo was hoisted for the whole world to see.

From the beginning of the Pepsi-Cola Company, efforts had been made to sell Pepsi throughout the world. In July 1985, Pepsi-Cola was consumed in space for the first time. A specialty can, designed to dispense Pepsi in zero gravity, was used aboard the space shuttle *Challenger*.

PepsiCo continued to expand by purchasing Kentucky Fried Chicken in 1987. This enlarged PepsiCo's restaurant system to more than 16,000 retail outlets. By 1989, Kentucky Fried Chicken had added $5 billion to PepsiCo sales.

*After serving for a year as president of the Pepsi Bottling Group,*

*Craig Weatherup became president of Pepsi-Cola in 1987.*

*To commemorate Pepsi's 1985 trip aboard the space shuttle*

*Challenger, the company issued a replica of the*

*can as a souvenir.*

# nothing else is a pepsi!

The 1990s began with Pepsi-Cola no longer being the cola challenger. In the previous decade, the company had proved itself as a major force in the soft drink business. So Pepsi continued to introduce new products and develop new packaging. The company's willingness to change had paid big dividends in sales and market shares, and the 1990s would be no exception.

In 1990, Pepsi's domestic soft drink sales reached $6.5 billion. Pepsi's success and growth would depend on how well the company enhanced the image of both new and existing brands. To remain an industry leader, the company had to not only maintain but build on the quality and reputation of the Pepsi trademark.

The executives who had led Pepsi into the '90s were beginning to retire, handing the company over to a new generation of leaders. The new leaders, such as Roger Enrico, who became chief executive officer of PepsiCo in 1996, had been part of the Pepsi Generation. They were given the responsibility of changing the company to meet future demand, as well as maintain-

ing the value of the Pepsi trademark.

By 1990, Pepsi and its related brands were available in nearly 150 countries, including the launching of Lehar Pepsi in India. Domestically, THE CHOICE OF A NEW GENERATION was still the Pepsi advertising theme. One promotion involved "cool cans." Introduced during the summer, these cans featured pop-art graphics, which made them collectible. The "cool can" promotion also offered cash prizes.

In 1990, Pepsi continued to buy up its franchises and incorporate them into the Pepsi Bottling Group. During the previous decade Pepsi had spent $4.6 billion in franchise acquisitions. The purpose was to increase efficiency and expand business, but owning a large number of former bottling franchises changed the structure of the Pepsi-Cola Company. Selling concentrate to bottlers

*Forming an alliance with Lipton Tea and Ocean Spray, Pepsi had become a "total beverage company."*

*The backup singers for Ray Charles, nicknamed the Uh-Huh Girls, became as popular as the commercials they appeared in. They traveled extensively to promote Pepsi.*

# PEPSI

own brands. This alliance capitalized on Pepsi's marketing and distribution skills to bring additional brand-name products to consumers—surveys showed that Americans, by a margin of almost two-thirds, prefer to buy well-known brands. Pepsi had become a major distributor of beverages, including colas, teas, fruit drinks, and isotonic beverages. The company adopted the motto "Total Beverage Company."

Over the years, Pepsi had developed a reputation for innovative commercials. Star power became the dominant theme in 1990, and the cast of celebrities appearing in Pepsi commercials included some of the biggest names in show business and sports. Now a veteran of the cola war commercials, Michael J. Fox returned for the fifth time in a spot entitled "Opera." Ray Charles made his debut in a Diet Pepsi commercial in 1990. Other celebrities included Kirk Cameron, Fred Savage, Joe Montana, and Magic Johnson, who became the first celebrity endorser to become part owner of a Pepsi franchise.

But not all of the commercials featured celebrities. In one of the most popular, called "Shady Acres," a delivery man mixes up his orders and takes Coke to a fraternity house and Pepsi to a retirement

*In the 1990s, Pepsi adopted a new logo for the first time in almost 20 years.*

was no longer Pepsi's primary concern. Instead, the company had to concentrate on operating a large bottling business; this dual role conflicted with the main purpose of the company.

With the cola market reaching the saturation point, and with American consumption of soft drinks reaching 48 gallons per person per year, Pepsi faced a dilemma. Should the company remain focused on the soft drink business, or should it look elsewhere for growth? Pepsi opted to pursue other ventures.

Americans were consuming more than 181 gallons of nonalcoholic beverages per year, and this offered Pepsi a greater potential market. In 1991, Pepsi formed an alliance with Lipton Tea and Ocean Spray to market those products, along with Pepsi's

*"Cool cans" became popular collectors' items, resulting in additional sales for Pepsi.*

The number-one rated, award-winning commercial, "Shady Acres," was one of Pepsi's most popular commercials.

home. The residents of the retirement home drink the Pepsi and are seen dancing and partying, while the Coke-drinking students at the fraternity house quietly play bingo. In a survey conducted by Opinion Research Corporation, Pepsi commercials were rated as America's favorites for the second year in a row, with "Shady Acres" ranking number one. The survey participants said that they particularly liked the way Pepsi was able to entertain while advertising.

In September 1991, after nearly 20 years without any major changes in the logo, Pepsi introduced a new look, along with new packaging graphics. The result of four years of research and development, the new graphics linked Pepsi and Diet Pepsi together in the consumer's mind. Research showed that the new packaging and graphics increased sales in food stores. The new logo did not completely abandon tradition because the bull's-eye portion was derived from the Pepsi crown logo introduced in 1943.

Pepsi's philosophy in the '90s had been sparked by company president Craig Weatherup's directive to focus efforts on the

consumer, thereby enabling Pepsi to meet consumer demands. This new philosophy was called "Right Side Up!"

Pepsi was on the scene when American troops were deployed for the Persian Gulf. As Operation Desert Storm began, Pepsi initiated Operation Desert Soda. The company distributed 10,000 cases of Pepsi and Diet Pepsi to military personnel to give them a taste of home. When the troops returned, Pepsi provided WELCOME HOME signs and free soda.

The success story for Pepsi advertising in 1991 involved Diet Pepsi commercials. The new jingle for Diet Pepsi, "You Got the Right One Baby, Uh-Huh," sung by Ray Charles and the "Uh-Huh Girls," became a hit. By the end of the year, the "Uh-huh" phrase became part of popular conversation. The commercial's successful run began during the Super Bowl. The USA Today ad meter, a consumer rating of commercials shown during the game, reported that Diet Pepsi had three of the top four commercials. One of the most popular was entitled "Audition"—in it celebrities and ordinary people alike audition to sing "You Got the Right

*In 1991, the packaging for Pepsi and Diet Pepsi received a makeover that featured the new logo.*

One Baby, Uh-Huh!" One reporter even said that the Ray Charles Diet Pepsi commercials were the high point of the Super Bowl.

After eight years and scores of awards, the CHOICE OF A NEW GENERATION advertising campaign was retired. In its place Pepsi introduced GOTTA HAVE IT. It was a return to product advertising. Instead of the New Generation being the center of Pepsi advertising, the spotlight was once again on Pepsi itself. GOTTA HAVE IT, introduced in 1992, emphasized the benefits of drinking Pepsi over the image of being a Pepsi drinker, and was linked to Pepsi's new graphics. One commercial actually showed a truck crashing into a billboard displaying the old logo and CHOICE OF A NEW GENERATION advertising. Pepsi's new look and new slogan were also featured in a commercial starring Cindy Crawford, marking the beginning of a long relationship between the supermodel and Pepsi-Cola.

The GOTTA HAVE IT slogan was introduced during the 1992 Super Bowl, Pepsi's favorite media event in which to premiere commercials. Pepsi spared no expense in hiring an all-star cast to make GOTTA HAVE IT a popular expression. Among the stars who appeared in the commercial were Yogi Berra, Regis Philbin, Bo Jackson, John Tesh, and Jimmy Connors.

*Time* magazine proclaimed the Diet Pepsi UH-HUH! campaign the best of 1991. Pepsi declared April 1992 Uh-Huh! Month, and sent one million cases of Diet Pepsi to Diet Coke drinkers. The Uh-Huh Girls became so popular that they made personal appearances without Ray Charles.

Pepsi was now offering an assortment of new beverages, including All Sport, an

*Returning to product-oriented advertising, Pepsi introduced the* GOTTA HAVE IT *slogan in 1992.*

and "Gotta Have It" are trademarks of PepsiCo, Inc.

Legendary musician Ray Charles made the phrase "You Got the Right One Baby, Uh-Huh!," part of American culture.

*Supermodel Cindy Crawford introduced Pepsi's new logo to the public.*

*Improved taste, the introduction of NutraSweet, and a big advertising campaign resulted in all-time high sales of Diet Pepsi during 1993.*

for the first time. Pepsi had been determined to continue taking risks, entering new markets and introducing new products. Throughout 1993, Pepsi continued to use the GOTTA HAVE IT slogan, combined with the phrase, BE YOUNG, HAVE FUN, DRINK PEPSI. This latter slogan became the dominant theme of the year's commercials and GOTTA HAVE IT was eventually abandoned because it was believed that it did not reach the target Pepsi drinker. BE YOUNG better fit the image of youth-oriented advertising that had begun with the original PEPSI GENERATION ads.

On the international market, Pepsi introduced a new drink called Pepsi Max in 1993. Pepsi Max is a low-calorie cola that is sweetened with a product that has not yet received FDA approval in the United States.

Diet Pepsi was still going strong in 1993 with the YOU GOT THE RIGHT ONE advertising campaign. Sales for the drink reached more than $4 billion. Ray Charles and the Uh-Huh Girls continued to endorse Diet Pepsi.

Pepsi literally hired its biggest celebrity endorser ever in 1994. Basketball star Shaquille O'Neal stands 7 feet 2 inches tall. O'Neal was used to introduce Pepsi's one-liter bottle called the Big Slam.

By 1995, the commercials shown during the Super Bowl had become almost as popular as the game itself. Competition for the best commercial during the Super Bowl led to a rivalry between advertising agencies. Pepsi aired two of the most talked-about commercials of 1995, which had also been rated the best of the Super Bowl. The number one commercial, "Boy Sucked Into Bottle," showed a boy so eager to get his last drop of Pepsi, that he ends up

isotonic sports drink used as a fluid replacement for athletes; H2Oh!, a sparkling water; and Avalon, a still water. Crystal Pepsi was introduced as a clear, caffeine-free, low-sodium cola with natural flavorings and no preservatives. The company had high expectations for the beverage, but sales declined after the initial interest wore off. Crystal Pepsi was withdrawn from the market, even though *Time* magazine had named it one of the 10 best new products of the year. The biggest problem with Crystal Pepsi may have been the consumer misperception that Crystal was simply a clear version of Pepsi.

Nineteen ninety-three saw Pepsi-Cola's worldwide profits reach more than $1 billion

being sucked into the bottle. The number two commercial depicted a Pepsi driver and a Coke driver fighting in a diner over a can of Pepsi.

The slogan NOTHING ELSE IS A PEPSI became the advertising theme for 1995. Pepsi advertising was again focused more on product than image. That same year, Pepsi celebrated the 30th anniversary of PepsiCo. In 30 years, the company had grown from $500 million in sales to more than $30 billion in sales. PepsiCo had grown from a company with a few products to one selling hundreds of products. PepsiCo now owned some of the most valuable trademarks in the world.

When Pepsi chairman Wayne Calloway retired in 1996 he was replaced by Roger Enrico. Calloway had been chairman since Don Kendall's retirement in 1986. Enrico, former president of Pepsi-Cola, is now responsible for leading Pepsi-Cola into its second century of business.

Enrico is best remembered for having capitalized on Coca-Cola's New Coke fiasco during the '80s. He knew how to beat Coke—Pepsi generated more than $10 billion in net sales in 1996.

Pepsi commercials again dominated the Super Bowl in 1996. And, as before, *USA Today*'s ad meter named Pepsi ads the top three spots shown during the game. The number one commercial depicted a Coke driver getting caught sneaking a can of Pepsi. Number two featured a hiker returning from the frozen tundra with a can of Pepsi frozen to his lips. When he walks into the doctor's office for treatment, he sees that everyone in the waiting room has the same problem. The number three commercial featured football and baseball player Deion Sanders in an animated spoof with the cartoon character Wile E. Coyote.

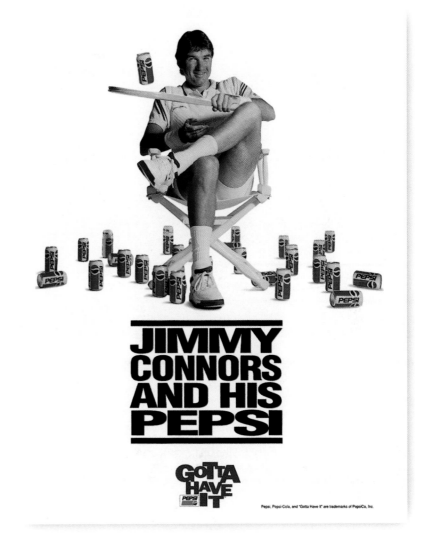

The 1996 PEPSI STUFF promotion was one of the company's most successful. Consumers collected points from Pepsi packaging and exchanged them for merchandise. More than 7 billion points were distributed; consumers could redeem their collected points for up to $125 million worth of Pepsi paraphernalia.

As in the past, challenges were presented to Pepsi-Cola and PepsiCo in 1997. Overseas bottling operations suffered severe setbacks in recent years, which cost Pepsi millions of dollars. The company is restructuring these operations to make them profitable.

In recent years, it became apparent to the management that the restaurant business

*The GOTTA HAVE IT commercials featured an all-star cast, including tennis pro Jimmy Connors.*

and the packaged goods business could not operate successfully under one company. Being in the restaurant business had actually hindered Pepsi-Cola's expansion into the fountain business. Because of the restaurants that PepsiCo owned, many of the other large restaurant chains recognized that Pepsi-Cola was in fact their competition, so these chains refused to sell Pepsi beverages at their restaurants. At the beginning of 1997, the PepsiCo board of directors approved the decision to spin off the restaurants into a separate company. In October 1997, the restaurant part of PepsiCo (Kentucky Fried Chicken, Taco Bell, and Pizza Hut) became Tricon Global Restaurants, Inc.

The new spin-off should enable PepsiCo to better focus on its two main businesses, Pepsi-Cola and Frito-Lay.

In 1997, Pepsi again produced the top-rated commercial at the Super Bowl. The number one spot featured bears dancing to a tune by the Village People. "Supermodels Love Baby," another Pepsi commercial, came in at number two. The 1997 slogan for Pepsi

*In 1992, Pepsi introduced Crystal Pepsi, a clear cola drink that was caffeine-free. It was designed for health-conscious consumers.*

*The biggest name in basketball, Shaquille O'Neal, became Pepsi's celebrity spokesperson in 1994.*

advertising was a return to the spirit of the Pepsi Generation—GENERATION NEXT.

Having survived two world wars, two bankruptcies, and competition that would have sunk many a company, Pepsi is entering its second century with the knowledge that success cannot be achieved by only having the best-tasting soft drink. A company must also have the best people—people willing to believe in the company and work toward pursuing the collective dream. With Coca-Cola's advantage basically evaporated, the playing field has been leveled, and Pepsi is ready for what will undoubtedly be known as The Pepsi Century. As Roger Enrico says in the Foreword to this book, "The first hundred years of Pepsi-Cola are just the opening chapter of a long and very exciting story."

The "Boy Sucked Into Bottle" commercial used sophisticated special effects to produce one of 1995's most popular commercials.

Believing that the slogan GOTTA HAVE IT did not appeal to youthful drinkers, Pepsi introduced BE YOUNG, HAVE FUN, DRINK PEPSI.

*In 1995, Pepsi switched to the slogan* NOTHING ELSE IS A PEPSI *and adopted the "Pepsi ball" as the new company symbol.*

# THE PEPSI SONG

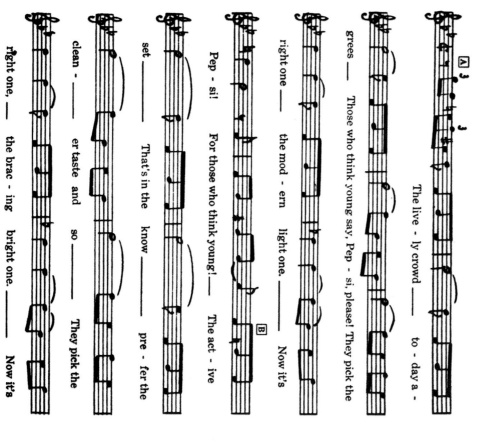

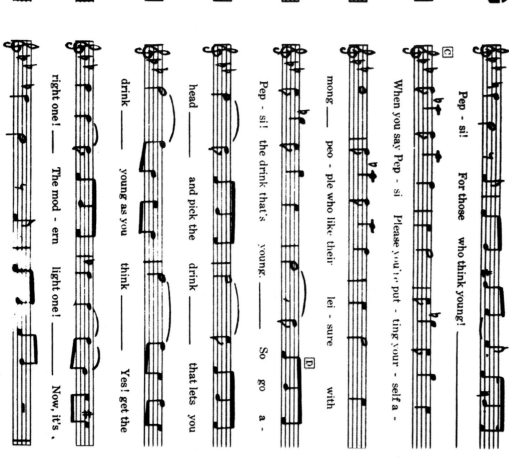

PEPSI COLA FORMULA:

| | | |
|---|---|---|
| Sugar- Standard Confectioners A | | 7500 pounds |
| Water, sufficient quantity to | | 1200 gallons |
| Caramel - burnt sugar color | | 12 gallons |
| Lime Juice | | 12 gallons |
| Phosphoric Acid S.G. 1.750 | | 58 pounds |
| Alcohol | 1/2/gallon | |
| Oil Lemon | 6 fluid ounces | |
| Oil Orange | 5 fluid ounces | |
| Cinnamon Oil | 4 fluid ounces | |
| Oil Nutmeg | 2 fluid ounces | |
| Oil Coriander | 2 fluid ounces | |
| Oil Petit Grain | 1 fluid ounce | |

Mix;   Stir two hours:

Boil Sugar and Water

(Signed)   C. D. Bradham, Chemist


U. S. Dist. Court )
                 )        In Re:  Pepsi Cola Co., Bankrupt
E. Dist., N. C.  )


I, Caleb D. Bradham, do solumnly swear that the foregoing is a true,
complete and correct formula for making or manufacturing "Pepsi
Cola" as heretofore made and manufactured and sold by the Pepsi
Cola Co., and is the formula for said Pepsi Cola as originated by me
and same is now the property of said Pepsi Cola Co., Bankrupt.


                         (Signed)  C. D. Bradham



Sworn to and subscribed before me
at New Bern, N. C., April 17, 1923, A. D.


                         Signed)  Joseph B. Cheshire, Jr.,

                         U. S. Referee in Bankruptcy